Information Security and Cryptography

More information about this series at http://www.springer.com/series/4752

Rosario Giustolisi

Modelling and Verification of Secure Exams

Springer

Rosario Giustolisi
Department of Computer Science
IT University of Copenhagen
Copenhagen, Denmark

ISSN 1619-7100   ISSN 2197-845X   (electronic)
Information Security and Cryptography
ISBN 978-3-030-09789-9   ISBN 978-3-319-67107-9   (eBook)
https://doi.org/10.1007/978-3-319-67107-9

Printed on acid-free paper

This Springer imprint is published by the registered company Springer International Publishing AG
part of Springer Nature.
The registered company address is: Gewerbestrasse 11, 6330 Cham, Switzerland

Foreword

We are endeavouring in the relocation of traditional human activities and facilities to the digital world: for example, electronic voting and its diverse security challenges still make researchers and developers alike tingle all over; electronic cash and its intricacies are there for the miners' rapture and, for just a little longer, the layman's bewilderment. If by *exams* we refer to all sorts of activities to verify and mark people's skills towards a degree, a post or a promotion, then this book convinces us that exams are following the same fate as voting or cash, getting an increasing level of computer support.

I was driven by love and respect for my job as an academic when, during 2004, I felt that the final exams of my Computer Security modules deserved the robustness and rigour of a security protocol. Hence, I designed WATA, the first version of the Written Authenticated Though Anonymous secure exam protocol, and soon started using a prototype profitably. Giustolisi chose the dawning challenges of that protocol and its variants as his main research and proficiently elaborated them out as the full-fledged research area and growing business value that secure electronic exams are today.

Although more and more universities are leafing through ways to modernise their exam systems, possibly with some use of computers, I still feel that electronic exams have various dimensions of uncertainty, such as whether they are to be taken on site or from home via the Internet, and then whether they are to be carried out over personal or institutional devices. The first contribution of this book is the design of a taxonomy that serves as a practical play board on which every exam type can be meaningfully positioned, hence understood with respect to its neighbours.

The security requirements of the various exam flavours are far from simple. While anonymous marking is intuitive because any honest candidate would like her test to be marked irrespectively of her identity, privacy steps in somewhat originally. For example, the mark of a candidate is meant to stay private in certain exams, and the candidate herself may be required to stay anonymous; however, the candidate will eventually need to prove her qualification, namely to confirm to someone, such as a lecturer or a boss, that she received a certain mark in a specific exam. Privacy therefore intertwines with universal verifiability, so that exam marks can be verified a posteriori.

The details of many exam protocols that are currently in use are easily accessible through the web. Surprisingly many can be found to insist on threat models that baffle a security protocol analyst, for example with their strong reliance on some bureaucrats' office to exercise the association between codes and candidates, or between codes and tests. Pseudo-anonymization cannot work without a real Chinese wall to confine the candidates' identities, while news scandals shout out that in practice those bureaucrats and the examiners might collude fraudulently or simply be members of the same family. By contrast, the protocols that follow below make a systematic effort to reduce the trust assumptions and rest on a realistic threat model.

I am very proud to be writing this foreword for a variety of reasons. The main one is the significance of the overarching topic that this book stands on. Exams are ubiquitous and required by qualifications at all levels; they are run virtually every minute somewhere in the world, perhaps more frequently than elections; they involve principals, such as candidates and examiners, who pose potentially contrasting security requirements that are not immutable over time. And finally, if democracy is strictly related to secure electronic voting, then meritocracy, which is one of the biggest attributes of democracy, proceeds from secure electronic exams.

Giampaolo Bella

Contents

List of Figures

List of Tables

Chapter 1

Introduction

Exams have a preeminent pedagogical role in teaching because they enable people to understand their skills and knowledge in a particular subject. Also, exams are the predominant way to establish meritocracy in modern societies. A record 2.115 million people applied for the yearly Chinese national service exam in 2016. They competed for 27,000 government posts, with a peak of 10,000 candidates running for a single job. It is worth noting that the idea to promote people based on exams came to the West only in the 17th century, when the British Empire began to hire employees using competitive exams to eliminate favouritism and corruption [KER09]. Today, many countries resort to tough exams for the qualification and selection of people in various areas that span from the education sector (e.g., admissions, coursework, and final qualifications) to the work sector (e.g., recruitment, progression, and professional qualifications). France is one of the countries that extensively uses exams, some of which are very competitive: the "Concours Général" is the most prestigious academic exam, which is taken by about 15,000 French students, and typically bears a success rate of less than 2% [Min14]; the exam to enter medicine studies attracts every year more than 50,000 candidates with a success rate of less than 15% [Fig14]. Exam meritocracy is one of the guiding principles in Singapore and is deemed to have contributed to the rapid growth of the country [Gop07].

Full meritocracy can be achieved only by fair exams. Straightening the exam procedures for the national service exam was one of the measures taken in China within the anti-corruption campaign started in 2012. Combating corruption threats already in the procedures that select government officers is, in fact, a clever starting point to avoid corrupted officers eventually. There are well-known methods that face possible threats. For example, threats ascribed to candidate cheating are typically mitigated by invigilation and anti-plagiarism methods. Candidate eligibility is enforced by invigilators by checking identity documents before allowing candidates to take the exam. Fair marking can be achieved by assigning a tracking number to candidate tests so that examiners can mark the tests while ignoring the authors.

The procedures outlined above are effective only if the authorities execute them correctly, namely candidate IDs are properly checked, tracking numbers are properly employed, and the author of a test is not revealed before the examiner marks it. However, authorities and examiners may be corrupted, and so they may commit transgressions that are harder to eradicate than transgres-

© Springer International Publishing AG 2018

R. Giustolisi, *Modelling and Verification of Secure Exams*, Information Security and Cryptography, https://doi.org/10.1007/978-3-319-67107-9_1

sions due to corrupted candidates. In the scandal known as the Atlanta Cheating [Cop13], about 35 people among school administrators, educators, and superintendents manipulated ranks and scores with the goal of gaining more school governmental funds. In early 2014, the BBC revealed a fraud on the UK visa system, in which the invigilator read out all the correct answers during the exam of English proficiency [Wat14]. More recently, a medical school admission exam scandal in India has resulted in thousands of arrests [New15]. The police revealed that candidates hired impersonators to take the written exam, and examiners gave higher marks to colluded candidates. The U.S. Navy disclosed cheating on the written exam that concerns the use of nuclear reactors that power carriers and subs [Lip14]. It was found that questions and answers had been illegally taken from a Navy computer since 2007 [Pre14].

The assistance of computers is becoming of critical importance for exams such that the main procedures of modern exams are carried out electronically. For example, Coursera, one of the most popular Massive Online Open Courses (MOOC), allows remote testing [Cou15, Cou12]. Also, the first step to becoming a permanent employee in one of the European Union agencies is to take a computer-based exam [Off13]. The use of computers simplifies certain tasks occurring during an exam but does not necessarily make the exam more secure. For example, the registration of a candidate for the exam and the notification of the mark via the Internet should be at least as secure as they would be face-to-face. Hence, we shall unfold the argument that an exam must be designed and analysed as carefully as security protocols normally are.

This book aims to shed light on the challenging security and privacy issues that modern exams face due to the assistance of computers. It follows that traditional threats and traditional deterrence strategies for exams should be reconsidered in the cyberspace environment. As threats may come from any of the roles being played in an exam, namely candidates and authorities may be corrupted to various extents, exams begin to look more balanced in terms of threats or benefits. The growth in the use of exam protocols has neither been followed nor preceded by a rigorous definition and analysis of their security. Hence, a fundamental step is to have a clear understanding of what the relevant security requirements are for exams. Without appropriate security notions, there is a risk to design flawed exams, which eventually makes people less confident of exam trustworthiness.

These concerns are relevant also for other domains, such as voting, and significant parts of the related work in this book highlight similarities and differences between exams and voting. We anticipate that a fundamental difference is that while fair elections aim to bring *democracy*, fair exams aim to bring *meritocracy* to societies. We observe that democracy is not meritocracy: in democracy, the selection of candidates is based on (people's) choices; in meritocracy, the selection of candidates is based on (the examiner's) assessment of their merit. Thus, understanding similarities and differences between exams and voting becomes an additional motivation of this book.

1.1   Objectives and Results

This work addresses three main objectives and aims at advancing the state of the art in the modelling and verification of secure exam protocols. A detailed description of this book's objectives is as follows.

Objective 1: Identify the relevant security requirements for exam protocols. This is a fundamental objective as it provides the basics for further research and determines the meaning of *secure* exam protocol. It requires the specification of a coherent terminology for exams including their phases and threat model. The outcome consists of a set of authentication, privacy, and verifiability requirements.

Objective 2: Develop a formal framework for the specification of security requirements and the analysis of exam protocols. This is a crucial objective that provides a rigorous and formal description of the security requirements for exams. It requires choosing a specific formalism in which the security requirements identified in Objective 1 can be expressed. The outcome is a flexible framework that is suitable for the modelling and analysis of exams.

Objective 3: Model secure protocols for different types of exams. This objective consists in proposing novel models for exam protocols that meet the security requirements according to the restrictions of the different exam types, which depend on the level of computer assistance and span from traditional to Internet-based exams. It requires combining secure cryptographic schemes to guarantee the often contrasting requirements. The outcome is a number of protocols that provide the same level of security though they belong to different exam types.

A first result of this work is a clear specification of the general building blocks of all exams, in terms of tasks, roles, phases, and threats. This paves the way for the definition of the security requirements for exams and facilitates the description of exam protocols.

A second result consists of two formal frameworks for the security analysis of exam protocols. The frameworks enable the study of authentication, privacy, and verifiability requirements, and support the specification of additional requirements. One framework enables the formalisation of authentication and privacy requirements in the applied π-calculus [AF01], while the other permits verifiability requirements to be specified in a more abstract model. Both frameworks are validated using ProVerif [Bla01] on computer-assisted and Internet-based exam protocols. The findings indicate that some protocols are flawed and prompt for modifications on their designs.

A last result consists of three exam protocols that guarantee a set of security requirements. The first protocol is for Internet-based exams and meets authentication, privacy, and verifiability requirements with minimal reliance on trusted parties. It distributes the trust across the servers that compose an *exponentiation mixnet*. The second protocol is for computer-assisted exams with face-to-face testing, and meets the requirements by means of lightweight participation of a trusted third party (TTP). It exploits the use of signatures and visual cryptography to ensure authentication and privacy in the presence of corrupted authorities and candidates. The third protocol eliminates the need for the TTP by combining oblivious transfer and visual cryptography schemes. It still ensures the same security requirements as the previous protocol's and supports a dispute resolution procedure without relying on a TTP.

The results of this research offer the basis for the modelling and verification of secure protocols for traditional, computer-assisted, and Internet-based exams.

1.2   Outline

This book is structured in seven chapters. In the following, we outline the contents of each chapter.

Chapter 2: Preliminaries and Definitions. This chapter introduces some terminology for exams and poses the foundations to formulate the security requirements. It begins with the description of the tasks that occur during an exam. In particular, it observes that levels of detail and abstraction of an exam specification constrain the number of tasks. The chapter continues by discussing the possible roles of an exam, possibly played by one or more principals. It identifies the typical phases, the basic threats coming from the main exam roles, and presents a taxonomy that classifies exams by types and categories. The chapter concludes with a description of the applied π-calculus and a preliminary formalisation of exam protocol.

Chapter 3: Security Requirements. This chapter contains the formal definitions of authentication, privacy, and verifiability requirements for exams. More specifically, it describes a framework based on the applied π-calculus for the specification of authentication and privacy, and a more abstract approach based on set-theory that enables the specification of verifiability. The latter consists of notions of *individual verifiability* as verifiability from the point of view of the candidate, and *universal verifiability* as verifiability from the point of view of an external auditor.

Chapter 4: The Huszti-Pethő Protocol. This chapter provides a first validation of the framework advanced in Chapter 3 through the ProVerif verification of the Huszti-Pethő exam protocol. It describes the protocol in great detail, studies its security, and concludes with a proposal that enhances the security of the protocol.

Chapter 5: The Remark! Internet-Based Exam. This chapter details *Remark!*, a protocol for Internet-based exams. It discusses the cryptographic building blocks on which Remark! is based, with a particular focus on the exponentiation mixnet. The chapter continues with the description of the protocol and the formal analysis in ProVerif of authentication, privacy, and verifiability requirements. Notably, it discusses how to map the abstract definitions of verifiability in ProVerif. The chapter concludes with some security considerations of Remark!.

Chapter 6: The WATA Family. This chapter focuses on *WATA*, a family of computer-assisted exams each employing some level of computer assistance though keeping face-to-face testing.   This chapter first introduces the early protocol versions of the protocols and reviews their security. Then, it details *WATA IV*, an exam protocol that meets more security requirements than the previous ones with less reliance on a TTP. WATA IV is then redesigned to meet the same security requirements without the need for any TTP. The chapter presents a detailed description of the enhanced version and a formal analysis in ProVerif, including the formalisation of an accountability requirement (Dispute Resolution). It concludes with a brief review of the protocols seen throughout the chapter.

Chapter 7: Conclusions. This chapter discusses the research presented throughout this work, outlines future work, and concludes the book.

Chapter 2

Preliminaries and Definitions

In this chapter, we introduce the fundamental elements of an exam system. We begin the treatment with an informal description of roles, principals, and threats, and conclude the chapter with the formal specification of these fundamental elements in the applied π-calculus. In consequence, describing and formalising a specific exam becomes easier at the sole price of further expanding or specifying these general concepts. We anticipate that we view an exam as a protocol that involves various tasks defining roles played by various principals through various phases. Hence, *exam*, *exam protocol*, or *exam system* are used interchangeably. With a security take, an exam is expected to withstand a threat model meeting a number of security requirements.

Outline of the chapter. Section 2.1 discusses the levels of detail and abstraction to characterise tasks. Section 2.2 introduces possible roles for exams and principals that play the exam roles. Section 2.3 identifies the typical phases of an exam. Section 2.4 details the potential security threats associated with the exam roles. Section 2.5 classifies exams by type and category. Section 2.7 outlines the basic constituents of the applied π-calculus. Section 2.8 introduces the formal framework by specifying the formal model of an exam.

2.1 Tasks

The ultimate goal of an exam is to assign a mark to a candidate. A number of *tasks* occur during an exam to fulfil that goal, such as generating the set of questions, building the tests, and marking them. We observe that the number of tasks cannot be fixed as it may change over two possible dimensions: the *level of detail* and the *level of abstraction* for the specification of the exam protocol.

The level of detail establishes whether a task should be explicitly mentioned or not. For example, the task of *sealing* the tests once they are generated might not be detailed in the specification of an exam. In security protocols, we often prescribe the task of *using* a nonce in a message, yet omitting the task of *fetching* it. Experience teaches us that a specification should make very clear (in)security assumptions about the protocol environment, otherwise the analysis may yield

© Springer International Publishing AG 2018
R. Giustolisi, *Modelling and Verification of Secure Exams*, Information Security and Cryptography, https://doi.org/10.1007/978-3-319-67107-9_2

debatable findings. In this vein, Needham stated that the public-key Needham-Schröder protocol considered the attacker as an outsider but never made this explicit [Nee02], a threat model that would remove the opportunity for Lowe's attack.

The level of abstraction establishes whether a task should be expanded into sub-tasks or not. For example, the task of generating the set of questions for the exam can be expanded into appointing question setters, setting the guidelines for wording and difficulty, etc. Similarly, in security protocols the task of fetching a nonce may be expanded into accessing a random number generator, running it, and receiving its output securely. These may be further expanded in turn.

From the security analysis standpoint, the levels of detail and of abstraction must be chosen with care in order to limit the necessary assumptions to realism and according to a threat model. For example, the details of generating the set of questions can be abstracted away if question setters are trusted, hence they keep secret the questions until after testing takes place. Conversely, such details should be explicitly described in case of a threat model that considers collusion between question setters and candidate. It follows that a threat model with less reliance on trusted parties normally requires a greater level of detail and abstraction for the specification of an exam than a threat model with more security assumptions. This is demonstrated in the following chapters and especially in Chapter 6, where the presence of trusted parties is progressively reduced in an exam protocol family series.

2.2   Roles and Principals

A *role* is a set of principals who perform a specific set, possibly of cardinality one, of tasks. During exams, an obvious role is the *candidate* role, of taking the exam to get a mark that may give the candidate a goal — such as obtaining a qualification, passing a periodical academic assessment, or being selected through a public examination. Of course, the candidate role could be specified, if needed, at a lower level of abstraction, and examples can be derived from actual protocol specifications. Other possible roles, also called *authority roles*, are as follows.

- The *registrar* role, of checking the eligibility of candidates who wish to take an exam, and of populating a list of registered candidates accordingly.

- The *question committee* role, of generating and building the tests, passing them to invigilators, forming the test answers in case of multiple-choice tests and passing them to the examiners.

- The *moderator* role, of setting the guidelines for wording and difficulty of questions, and liaising with the question committee to independently ensure that the tests conform to the guidelines as well as readability and appropriateness standards.

- The *invigilator* role, of distributing tests to candidates, of checking candidates' identities, of following candidates while they take their test preventing them from misbehaving.

- The *collector* role, of collecting the tests from the candidates at the end of the exam time, and distributing the test answers to the examiners.

- The *examiner* role, of reading the test answers and of producing adequate marks for them.

- The *recorder* role, of keeping records of what candidates received what marks at the exam.

- The *notifier* role, of informing the candidates of the marks that their respective tests received, and of storing this information with some recorders.

It can be seen that each authority role clearly indicates its set of tasks, demonstrating the levels of detail and of abstraction that we advocate. If an exam features an additional task, then this could either extend an existing role or form a new role. Also, in order to meet some requirements, an exam may allow two or more roles to merge into one, or may prescribe splitting a role into two or more. For example, the role of question committee can be split into exam convener, question setter, and question reviewer, as practised in some universities. Typically, candidate and authority roles cannot be merged (and still meet the requirements), except with exams such as MOOC [YP13], where homework is peer-reviewed, namely candidates mark each other.

Exams see the participation of a number of *principals*, each playing one or more of the roles defined above. Principals may change depending on the specific exam, and various examples can be made.

At university, the candidate role is played by students, while the roles of invigilator, collector and examiner are sometimes played by a single lecturer. At an extreme, there are only two principals, with a student as a candidate and a lecturer playing all authority roles. Today, ProctorU [Inc15] invigilates via webcams the candidates who take exams from home. At public examinations, the police could take the invigilator role.

Principals are not necessarily humans. They may as well be pieces of software playing various roles, such as invigilator, by filming candidates during testing, or examiner, by marking multiple-choice tests mechanically.

Irrespective whether they are human or not, it must be assumed that principals may act somewhat maliciously. We anticipate that such assumptions are fundamental when considering corrupted principals in the formal definition of our security requirements. In fact, they will define a threat model, as we shall see below.

2.3   Phases

We identify the four main phases that typically take place sequentially during an exam. They will be further detailed and specified by actual exams in the remainder of this book.

- At *preparation*, certain authorities, typically registrars, file a new exam, and check the standard eligibility criteria, such as correct payment of fees and adequate previous qualifications, of candidates who wish to take the exam. Only those who satisfy the criteria shall be successfully registered, and the authorities ultimately produce a list of candidates registered for the exam. Similarly, the authorities might produce a list of eligible examiners. Most importantly, this phase includes the preparation of tests and all the relevant material for the subsequent phase. For instance, creation of questions, printing of tests, and generation of pseudonyms to anoymise tests are tasks accomplished in this phase. The type of exam (e.g., traditional, computer-assisted, Internet-based, etc.), the category of exam (i.e., written, oral, or performance), and the form of exam (e.g., multiple choice, short answer, essay, etc.) condition the preparation of tests.

- At *testing*, each registered candidate gets a test containing a number of questions, which were previously built by authorities, normally the question committee and moderators. Other authorities, typically invigilators, watch candidates through this phase. Each candidate answers their test, and may have to complete it with their personal details. The candidate then submits their test answers to an authority, such as an invigilator.

- At *marking*, the test answers of all candidates reach the examiner authority for evaluation. More precisely, the authority reads the test answers and evaluates their adherence to the required knowledge, then forming a mark, chosen on a given scale, for each test. Some real-world example scales are: pass/fail, A to E, 60% to 100%, and 18 to 30. With multiple-choice tests, the examiner authority could be a computer program.

- At *notification*, an authority, commonly a notifier, gives each candidate the mark for the test answers the candidate submitted; either beforehand or afterwards, the notifier also stores this information with a recorder, commonly a server equipped with a DBMS.

Any subset of phases may either take place *on site*, with candidates meeting the authorities face-to-face or *off site*. Regulated by the specific application requirements, these features will shape the exam experience.

Moreover, any subset of these phases may take place either traditionally, namely by pen and paper, or on computer. For example, we observed above that marking can be easily computer assisted with multiple-choice tests; similarly, notification could take place via dedicated workstations installed in the exam site.

The specification of the exam phases clarifies the terminology that is used coherently throughout this book, but it may be useful to the reader if we point out that various synonyms are used in the literature. For example, "registration" or "setup" may refer to the preparation phase; "examination" is often taken to indicate the testing phase; "evaluation" or "grading" may indicate the marking phase; "exam", "examination", or "assessment" may sometimes even refer to the full sequence of phases.

2.4   Threats

A number of threats could be envisaged against exams, and some basic threats are enumerated here.

Threats may derive from each task. For example, even the task of printing may invite the principal who performs it to alter the printout or not print at all. We assume each principal to be rational in the sense that the principal does not misbehave unless there is a clear benefit for them or, in case of *collusion*, for another principal.

We conveniently define threats on a per-role basis. Therefore, augmenting a role with additional tasks would require extending the role-specific threats; adding new roles formed of new tasks would require extending the threats over the role; merging roles would yield the union of the threats of the original roles; splitting a role would partition its threats enabling each formed role to pose the threats deriving from its tasks.

We define some basic threats coming from the preeminent roles used in the rest of this book: the candidate, the authority, and the *observer* roles. The observer role has no specific tasks in an exam, hence it is not in the list of roles outlined above. An observer can be the public in open-door testing as well as software (e.g., a spyware) in a computer that is used for the exam.

A specific protocol shall customise the list of the threats according to its roles.

The threat model is the standard Dolev-Yao [DY83] over the roles (or their portions) that are impersonated by computer programs. Additionally, the roles (or their portions) that are impersonated by humans pose the threats detailed below.

The corrupted candidate performs any tasks in order to:

- register for an exam without being eligible;

- register on behalf of someone else;

- answer their test with knowledge obtained by cheating;

- get a higher mark than what the examiner assigns to their test.

These threats are significant. Eligibility criteria may be stringent, such as payment of fees and restricted participation to certain exam dates, hence the interest in misbehaviour. Candidates' attempts at cheating, for example by consulting books, and at getting a better mark than theirs are well known. In particular, the latter may see a candidate send someone else, more knowledgeable than them, to sit for the exam on the candidate's behalf, or see a candidate swap their mark with that of another candidate known to be very knowledgeable. Thus candidates may collude with each other to achieve their goal. It can be anticipated that these threats demand effective authorisation, authentication, invigilation, and marking procedures.

The corrupted authority performs any tasks in order to:

- assign an unfair mark to a specific candidate, namely to over-mark or under-mark her, or assign no mark at all.

This is the fundamental threat authorities may pose to candidates. This threat may hinder students' spontaneity during university lectures. This threat is well known in academic conferences, and is partially addressed with blind reviews. More seriously it has also brought corruption into public competitions. Arguably, it calls for anonymous marking, verifiability, and accountability requirements.

The observer performs any tasks in order to:

- gather any private information.

Observers may be allowed to watch parts of the exam, typically the candidates while they take their tests, to promote transparency and raise public acceptance of the regularity of procedures. They may, however, have malicious intentions and seek out any form of private information such as candidates' questions and marks. If the exam is somewhat assisted by computers or by the Internet, then this threat becomes a digital one.

2.5   Taxonomy

Having seen the phases of an exam, we can specify the dictionary definition of the word "exam" conveniently for our purposes.

Definition 1 (Exam) *An exam is a formal test taken to show a candidate's knowledge of a subject. It comprises the four sequential phases* preparation, testing, marking *and* notification.

Definition 1 only specifies the main functional requirement of an exam, that candidates take the exam. It purposely omits additional functional requirements that may depend on the application scenario, such as that candidates be allowed to register from home.

2.5.1   Exam Types

Exams can be classified in various types according to the following definitions.

Definition 2 (Computer-assisted exam) *A* computer-assisted exam *is an exam such that at least one of its phases receives some level of assistance from computers or Information Technology.*

At first glance, Definition 2 appears to be too wide to the extent that every exam is a computer-assisted exam. For example, an exam that only requires computers to edit the questions could be classified as computer-assisted. However, as observed in Section 2.1, the levels of detail and abstraction for the specification of the protocol should be considered to find the correct classification of the exam. Thus, if the way the questions are edited is not explicitly mentioned in the description of the protocol, the exam should not be classified as computer-assisted. A qualifying example of a computer-assisted exam is to allow candidates to register from home, but then continuing traditionally, namely fully on paper and without the use of computers.

Definition 3 (Traditional exam or non-computer-assisted exam) *A* traditional exam *is an exam such that none of its phases receives any level of assistance from computers or Information Technology in general. A traditional exam is also said to be a* non-computer-assisted exam *to indicate the absence of computer assistance.*

Definitions 2 and 3 insist that exams can be partitioned between computer-assisted and traditional exams depending on computer assistance. Having seen the main partition within exams, various types of e-exams can be defined. For brevity, it is useful to refer to the acronyms in Table 2.1.

NCA	non-computer-assisted
CA	computer-assisted
CB	computer-based
IA	Internet-assisted
IB	Internet-based

Table 2.1: Acronyms for exam types

Definition 4 (Computer-based exam) *A* computer-based exam *is an exam whose testing phase takes place fully on a computer.*

We decide to pivot Definition 2 around the testing phase because an exam is often somewhat simplistically understood as that phase alone in practice. The definition insists that the testing phase of a CB exam takes place fully on computer, ruling out exams where questions are given orally or are written on a board, which would only be CA exams. Clearly, a CB exam also is a CA exam but not vice versa.

Definition 5 (Internet-assisted exam) *An* Internet-assisted exam *is an exam such that at least one of its phases receives some level of assistance from the Internet.*

It is logical that Definition 2 and Definition 5 have the same structure, and similar considerations about levels of detail and abstraction apply here. Definition 5 requires some use of the Internet in some phases. For example, an exam that only relies on the Internet to notify the candidates of their marks would be an IA exam. Clearly, an IA exam also is a CA exam. An IA exam may also be, but not necessarily, a CB exam. From a set-theory standpoint, if $\mathcal{CB}$ is the set of all CB exams, and $\mathcal{IA}$ is the set of all IA exams, it follows that $\mathcal{CB}$ and $\mathcal{IA}$ intersect but do not coincide.

Definition 6 (Internet-based exam) *An* Internet-based exam *is an exam whose testing phase takes place fully over the Internet.*

The formulation of Definition 6 closely maps one of Definition 4. Clearly, an IB exam is also an IA exam; an IB exam must also be a CB exam because the testing phase could not happen fully over the Internet without happening fully over some computer (or similar devices such as smartphones).

Also, Definition 5 and Definition 6 purposely omit the specification of the venue where the exam phases happen, whether locally, at the hosting institution's premises, or remotely from the candidate's place. For example, even an IB exam could happen locally.

Having defined the various types of exams, the main building blocks for our taxonomy of exams are available. Still, for each exam type, it is useful to define the set of all exams of that type, as Table 2.2 does in a self-explaining form. Now, the exam taxonomy can be introduced using a set-theory notation; it is in Figure 2.1, and demonstrates the relations discussed above between the various exam types.

As anticipated above, all roles span uniformly across the entire taxonomy because principals can either be human or not. Other objects may have to be re-interpreted depending on the exam type. For example, a test consists of some

$$\begin{array}{c|l}
\mathcal{NCA} & \text{set of all NCA exams} \\
\mathcal{CA} & \text{set of all CA exams} \\
\mathcal{CB} & \text{set of all CB exams} \\
\mathcal{IA} & \text{set of all IA exams} \\
\mathcal{IB} & \text{set of all IB exams}
\end{array}$$

Table 2.2: Sets of exam types

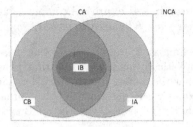

Figure 2.1: A set-theory representation of exams

paper (showing questions and, later, answers) for all exams in $\mathcal{NCA}$, of some file(s) for all exams in $\mathcal{CB}$, of either some paper or some file(s) for all exams in $\mathcal{CA} \setminus \mathcal{CB}$.

The taxonomy in Figure 2.1 seems to bear potential to capture more general scenarios than just exams, and precisely those commonly addressed as *collaborative working environment* [FJ95]. However, one would need to map the exam phases identified above to the main phases of other scenarios, and this exceeds the aims of the present research.

2.5.2   Exam Categories

Exams can be categorised as *written exams*, *oral exams*, or *performance exams*, as outlined below. Written exams are usually preferred when the number of candidates is high. Oral exams are considered the most effective practice to assess knowledge, but examiners tend to mark candidates less objectively compared to written exams. Performance exams are impractical when many candidates need to be evaluated.

Our taxonomy was built to reflect written exams, where testing takes place in writing, namely with questions and answers given using various combinations of reading and (hand- or type-)writing on paper, boards, screens, etc. However, our taxonomy can be stretched out to reflect also oral and performance exams as explained in the following, although this exceeds the scope of this book.

Oral exams see questions and answers given orally, either synchronously by interviews or asynchronously by some proxying. Synchronous exams can be represented by our taxonomy, as one can easily realise by looking at Figure 2.1 with synchronous oral exams in mind. For example, a synchronous oral exam in $\mathcal{IB}$ may have the testing phase via videoconferencing; even one in the set $\mathcal{CB} \setminus \mathcal{IA}$ makes perfect sense if recording the interview is required.

Also asynchronous oral exams comply with our taxonomy. Through the use of techniques of speech processing or audio sampling, asynchronous oral exams could have the testing phase via voice chats. Also, in this case exams in $\mathcal{CB} \setminus \mathcal{IA}$ are valuable, by yielding the full chat history of the testing. Envisaging an asynchronous oral exam that is NCA requires admitting the role of proxy to be played by a human without any computer assistance. If this is deemed impractical or implausible, then the taxonomy could be easily pruned of the NCA part, only for the category of asynchronous oral exams.

Performance exams differ from oral exams because the former require a candidate to actually perform an activity, rather than answer questions orally. The same techniques envisaged for synchronous and asynchronous oral exams (e.g., videoconferencing, audio sampling, speech processing) hold for performance exams as well as the considerations that regard the exam types.

There may also be *hybrid exams*, for instance, where testing combines written and oral means: a lecturer could dictate the questions for candidates to answer in writing. Although it might be less popular than written or oral exams, we argue that this category too could be represented with our taxonomy, perhaps with minor adjustments.

2.6   Exams as Security Protocols

We have seen that the fundamental elements of an exam are roles, principals, and tasks. These elements can be naturally found in communication protocols where roles (e.g., initiator, responder), principals (e.g., Alice, Bob), and tasks (e.g., send a nonce, insert a record in a database) establish the set of formal rules that describe how computers exchange messages over a network. The presence and the preeminence of threats require us to consider and study exams as *security* protocols.

Security protocols are distributed algorithms that use cryptography to achieve some security requirements.

The design of such protocols can be a difficult task that might lead to serious security flaws. The literature is full of security protocols and standards that have been demonstrated to be bugged [CJS+07, HM05, BGW01], a trend that is unlikely to change [ACC+08, AMRR14]. Formal approaches for the analysis of security protocol have been successfully used to discover security flaws, such as the famous one in the Needham-Schroeder Public Key protocol [Low96], and eventually helped in fixing the protocols with some level of guarantee. Experience shows that formal approaches are important also in the design phase of protocols as they force designers to have a deep understanding of their models and what they aim to achieve. The study of security of exam systems should not be dispensed by formal approaches. Similar to other systems like voting and auction, exams have not been designed with security in mind. This is problematic since the recent growth in the use of exam protocols has not been followed, nor preceded, by a rigorous understanding and analysis of their security. Although there are recent proposals for exam protocols with a security-by-design approach [HP10, CRHJDJ06, HPC04, BCCKR11], no formal analyses have been conducted against these proposals. Since almost all the existing exam protocols normally assume trusted authorities, only a small set of requirements, namely the ones concerning authentication of candidates, are usually considered in the analysis. As already noted in the previous chapter, exam authorities can be corrupted as can candidates, and exam protocols should consider a larger set of requirements including privacy.

Security protocols have been historically analysed with two different approaches, one based on the symbolic model, and one based on computational complexity theory. Symbolic analysis methods for protocol analysis find their root in the seminal works of Needham and Schroeder [NS78] and Dolev and Yao [DY83], which assume perfect cryptography and an unbounded active attacker who controls the entire network. Formal logic and automated tools based on the symbolic model have been used successfully to analyse security protocols.

Methods based on computational complexity theory were initially developed by Goldwasser and Micali [GM84]. Analysis in the computational model usually sees the attacker as a polynomial probabilistic Turing machine. Such analysis is deemed to be more realistic because it avoids the perfect cryptography assumption, and thus provides more insights about vulnerabilities of security protocols: an attack in the symbolic model leads to an attack in the computational model, while the contrary is not true in general. However, methods based on computational complexity theory are harder to mechanise (only recently mechanised tools have been proposed to assist manual proofs [Bla08, BGZB09]) and are not suitable for automation. Proofs are mostly manual and difficult as they involve reasoning about probability and computational complexity, and are hence prone to human errors. We thus choose to develop the formal framework for exams using the symbolic model.

The symbolic model.   Several symbolic techniques have been proposed over the last 25 years. Merritt [Mer83] proposed to describe protocols by rewrite rules. Burrows *et al.* [BAN90] introduced the so-called *BAN logic* to reason about authentication requirements. Meadows [Mea96] proposed a language based on events for specifying security protocols, and introduced the *NRL Analyzer*, a model checker capable of verifying authentication and secrecy requirements. Ryan and Schneider [RS00] pioneered the idea of using process algebras for the analysis of security protocols. In Hoare's CSP [Hoa78, Sch98] the protocol's principals are naturally modelled as processes, while security requirements are modelled as reachability properties. Paulson [Pau98] introduced the *Inductive Approach* wherein principals are modelled as a set of rules that inductively define an unbounded set of traces. A protocol guarantees a security requirement if the requirement inductively holds for all possible traces. Thayer [F99] proposed the strand spaces approach, which features an intuitive way to reason about traces generated by the security protocols: a strand is a sequence of events in which a protocol's principal may participate. Abadi and Gordon [AG97] introduced the spi-calculus, a process algebra that extends the π-calculus [MPW92] with explicit representation of cryptographic operations. The next section details the applied π-calculus [AF01], which extends further the spi-calculus with a richer algebra for the modelling of cryptographic primitives.

2.7   The Applied π-calculus

The applied π-calculus [AF01] is a formal language for the description and analysis of security protocols, in which principals are represented as processes. Its syntax consists of *names*, *variables*, and *signatures*. The latter are function symbols each with an arity. Names represent channels and data, while function symbols represent cryptographic primitives such as encryption, decryption, digital signature, and hash functions. Function symbols applied to names and variables generate *terms*. Tuples of arity l, such as $n_1, \ldots, n_l$, can be abbreviated in $\tilde{n}$.

Equational theories. Whereas the π-calculus supports only a fixed set of cryptographic primitives, the applied π-calculus allows one to model user-defined primitives by means of *equational theories*. An equational theory E describes the equations that hold on terms built from the signature. Terms are related by an equivalence relation $=$ induced by E. For instance, the equation $dec(enc(m, pk(k)), k) = m$ models an asymmetric encryption scheme. The term m is the message, the term k is the secret key, the function $pk(k)$ models the corresponding public key, the term enc models the encryption function, and the term dec models the decryption function.

Processes. The grammar for *plain* processes is outlined in Figure 2.2. The null process 0 does nothing; the process $P|Q$ is the parallel composition of processes P and Q; the process $!P$ behaves as an unbounded number of copies of processes P running in parallel; the process $\nu n.P$ generates a new *private* name n, then behaves like P; the conditional process 'if $m = m'$ then P else Q' behaves like the process P if $m = m'$ and like the process Q otherwise. For brevity, one can omit sub-term 'else Q' when Q is 0; the process $in(u, x).P$ awaits for an input from channel u, then behaves as the process P with the received message replacing the variable x; Finally, the process $out(u, m).P$ outputs the message m on the channel u, then behaves as the process P. For brevity, one can omit $.P$ when the process P is 0.

$P, Q, R ::=$	plain processes
0	null process
$P|Q$	parallel composition
$!P$	replication
$\nu n.P$	name restriction (new)
if $m = m'$ then P else Q	conditional
$in(u, x).P$	message input
$out(u, m).P$	message output

Figure 2.2: The grammar for plain processes in the applied π-calculus

The grammar for *extended* processes is outlined in Figure 2.3. Extended processes model the knowledge exposed to the attacker. An *active substitution* $\{^m/_x\}$ is a process that replaces the variable x with the term m. We refer to a substitution also with σ. We use $m\sigma$ to refer to the result of applying σ to m. The sets $fv(A)$, $bv(A)$, $fn(A)$ and $bn(A)$ respectively include free variables, bound variables, free names, and bound names of the process A. An extended process is *closed* if all variables are bound or defined by an active substitution.

The definition of *corrupted process* [DKR06] is useful to model corrupted principals who actively collaborate with the attacker.

The definition outlined below specifies how to transform a process into a corrupted process. This transformation is based on two channels c_1 and c_2, which the process uses to receive and send data to the attacker.

$A, B, C ::=$	extended processes
P	plain process
$A\|B$	parallel composition
$!P$	replication
$\nu n.A$	name restriction
$\nu x.A$	variable restriction
$\{^m/_x\}$	active substitution

Figure 2.3: The grammar for extended processes in the applied π-calculus

Definition 7 (Corrupted process P^{c_1,c_2}) *Let P be a plain process and c_1, c_2 be two channel names such that $c_1, c_2 \notin fn(P) \cup bn(P)$. The corrupted process P^{c_1,c_2} is defined as follows:*

- $0^{c_1,c_2} \doteq 0$,

- $(P|Q)^{c_1,c_2} \doteq P^{c_1,c_2}|Q^{c_1,c_2}$,

- $(!P)^{c_1,c_2} \doteq !P^{c_1,c_2}$,

- $(\nu n.P)^{c_1,c_2} \doteq \nu n.out(c_1, n).P^{c_1,c_2}$ *if n is a name of base type, otherwise* $(\nu n.P)^{c_1,c_2} \doteq \nu n.P^{c_1,c_2}$,

- *(if $m = m'$ then P else Q)$^{c_1,c_2} \doteq in(c_2, x).if\ x = true\ then\ P^{c_1,c_2}\ else$ Q^{c_1,c_2} where x is a fresh variable and true is a constant,*

- $(in(u, x).P)^{c_1,c_2} \doteq in(u, x).out(c_1, x).P^{c_1,c_2}$ *if x is a variable of base type, otherwise* $(in(u, x).P)^{c_1,c_2} \doteq in(u, x).P^{c_1,c_2}$,

- $(out(u, m).P)^{c_1,c_2} \doteq in(c_2, x).out(u, x).P^{c_1,c_2}$, *where x is a fresh variable.*

A *frame* is an extended process built from 0 and active substitutions of the form $\{^m/_x\}$ by parallel composition and restriction. We use Φ and Ψ to range over frames. The domain $dom(\Phi)$ of a frame Φ is the set of the variables for which Φ defines a substitution. Every extended process A can be mapped to a frame $\Phi(A)$ by replacing every plain process in A with 0. The frame $\Phi(A)$ can be seen as a representation of the knowledge of the process to its environment.

Finally, a *context* is an extended process C with a hole, written $C[\_]$. It can be used to represent the environment in which the process is run.

Reachability and Correspondence Properties

In the applied π-calculus, secrecy can be modelled as a reachability property. The secrecy of a term m is preserved if an attacker, defined as an arbitrary process, cannot construct m from any run of the protocol. The definitions of *name distinct*, and *reachability-based secrecy* [RS11] models secrecy. A name-distinct process signifies that the names mentioned in a term appear unambiguously in the process either as free or bound names. The definition of reachability-based secrecy says that an attacker cannot build a process A that can output the secret term m.

Definition 8 (name-distinct for $\tilde{m}$) *A plain process P is name-distinct for a set of names $\tilde{m}$ if $\tilde{m} \cap fn(P) \cap bn(P) = \emptyset$ and for each name $n \in \tilde{m} \cap bn(P)$ there is exactly one restriction νn in P.*

Definition 9 (Reachability-based secrecy) *A plain process P that is name-distinct for the names mentioned in the term m* preserves *reachability-based secrecy if there is no plain process A such that* $(fn(A) \cup bn(A)) \cap bn(P) = \emptyset$ *and* $P|A$ *can output m.*

In the applied π-calculus, authentication can be defined using *correspondence assertions* [WL93]. An event e is a message emitted into a special channel that is not under the control of the attacker. Events may contain arguments $M_1, ... M_n$, which are never revealed to the attacker. Events do not change the behaviour of the process in which they are located, but normally flag important steps in the execution of the protocol. To model correspondence assertions, we annotate processes with events such as $e\langle M_1, ... M_n \rangle$ and reason about the relationships ($\rightsquigarrow$) between events and their arguments in the form *"if an event* $e\langle M_1, ... M_n \rangle$ *has been executed, then event* $e'\langle N_1, ... N_n \rangle$ *has been previously executed"*, which is formalised as the following definition.

Definition 10 (Correspondence assertion) *A correspondence assertion is a formula of the form* $e\langle M_1, ... M_i \rangle \rightsquigarrow e'\langle N_1, ... N_j \rangle$.

By adding the keyword *inj*, it is possible to model an injective correspondence assertion, which signifies that *"if an event* $e\langle M_1, ... M_n \rangle$ *has been executed, then a distinct earlier occurrence of event* $e'\langle N_1, ... N_n \rangle$ *has been previously executed"*.

Definition 11 (Injective correspondence assertion) *An injective correspondence assertion is a formula of the form* $e\langle M_1, ... M_i \rangle \rightsquigarrow inj\ e'\langle N_1, ... N_j \rangle$.

Authentication is only one of the requirement that can be modelled by correspondence assertions. Correspondence assertions can, for instance, capture also verifiability requirements, as we shall see in Chapter 5.

Observational Equivalence

The notion of observation equivalence can capture privacy requirements. Informally, two processes are observational equivalent if an observer cannot distinguish the processes despite the fact that they might handle different data or perform different computations. To formalise observational equivalence, we first introduce the notion of *internal reduction* ($\rightarrow$), which captures the evolution of a process with respect to communication and conditionals as:

- $out(c, x).P | in(c, x).Q \rightarrow P|Q$;

- if $n = n$ then P else $Q \rightarrow P$;

- if $l = m$ then P else $Q \rightarrow Q$, where L and m are not equivalent.

Definition 12 (Observational equivalence) Observational equivalence *(≈) is the largest symmetric relation* $\mathcal{R}$ *on extended processes such that A* $\mathcal{R}$ *B implies:*

1. if $A \rightarrow^* C[out(c, M).P]$, *then* $B \rightarrow^* C[out(c, M).P]$;

2. if $A \rightarrow^* A'$, *then* $B \rightarrow^* B'$ *and* $A' \mathcal{R} B'$ *for some* B';

3. $C[A] \mathcal{R} C[B]$ *for all context* $C[\_]$.

The relation $\rightarrow^*$ expresses the transitive and reflexive closure of the relation $\rightarrow$. Definition 12 says that two processes A and B are observational equivalent if: 1. the process A evolves to a process that can output on channel c, also B can evolve to a similar process; 2. if A evolves to some process A', also B can evolve to some process B', and A' and B' are observational equivalent; 3. for all contexts, $C[A]$ and $C[B]$ are observational equivalent.

The definition of observational equivalence is impracticable because it requires the quantification over contexts. To avoid quantification over contexts, we first introduce the definitions of *equality of terms* and *static equivalence*. The latter captures the static part of observational equivalence as it only examines the current state of the processes. Then, we formalise *labelled bisimilarity*, which captures the dynamic behaviour of the processes and is equivalent to observational equivalence. In fact, Abadi and Fournet [AF01] proved that observational equivalence and labelled bisimilarity coincide.

Definition 13 (Equality of terms) *Two terms m and m' are equal in the frame Φ, written $(m = m')\Phi$, if $\Phi \equiv \nu\tilde{n}.\sigma$, $m\sigma = m'\sigma$ and $\{\tilde{n}\} \cap (fn(m) \cup fn(m')) = \emptyset$, for some names $\tilde{n}$ and some substitution σ.*

Definition 14 (Static equivalence) *Two closed frames Φ and Ψ are statically equivalent, written $\Phi \approx_s \Psi$, if $dom(\Phi) = dom(\Psi)$, and for all terms m and m' we have that $(m = m')\Phi$ if and only if $(m = m')\Psi$. Two extended processes A and B are statically equivalent, written $A \approx_s B$ if their frames are statically equivalent.*

In fact, two processes are statically equivalent if all their previous operations gave the same results so that they cannot be distinguished from the messages they exchange with the environment.

Definition 15 (Labelled bisimilarity)
Labelled bisimilarity *($\approx_l$) is the largest symmetric relation $\mathcal{R}$ on extended processes, such that $A \mathcal{R} B$ implies:*

1. *$A \approx_s B$*

2. *if $A \rightarrow^* A'$, then $B \rightarrow^* B'$ and $A' \mathcal{R} B'$ for some B'*

3. *if $A \xrightarrow{\alpha} A'$, $fv(\alpha) \subseteq dom(A)$ and $bn(\alpha) \cap fn(B) = \emptyset$, then $B \rightarrow^* \xrightarrow{\alpha} \rightarrow^* B'$ and $A'\mathcal{R}B'$ for some B'.*

The relation $A \rightarrow^\alpha A'$ defines a labelled semantics that avoids the quantification over the contexts. It signifies that A can evolve to A' using a labelled transition. This happens when A performs an input or an output due to some interaction with the environment, and α is the label standing for the involved action.

2.8   Modelling Exams Formally

The applied π-calculus allows us to describe roles, principals, and tasks of an exam. Roles and tasks can be modelled as processes in the applied π-calculus. These processes communicate via public or private channels, and can create fresh random values, which can serve as keys or nonces, for example. Processes can perform tests and cryptographic operations, which are functions on terms with respect to an equational theory describing some algebraic properties.

Principals can be modelled via substitutions applied to processes in the applied π-calculus. A substitution associates a particular principal to a role (process) that it runs. In fact, substitutions realise an *instance* of an exam protocol.

The threat model of an exam protocol consists of a Dolev-Yao attacker who has full control of the network, namely of the public channels. The attacker can also inject messages of his choice into the public channels, and exploit the algebraic properties of cryptographic primitives due to an equational theory. Moreover, the ability of the attacker can be extended with corrupted principals according to Definition 7. However, the attacker has no control of private channels, which are normally used to model out-of-band communications between processes. The attacker cannot even know if any communication happens over private channels. Thus, he can eavesdrop, drop, substitute, duplicate, and delay messages that principals send one another over public channels.

Having seen the basic constituents of the applied π-calculus, we can provide the definition of *exam protocol* according to the calculus.

Definition 16 (Exam protocol) *An* exam protocol *is a tuple* $(C, E, Q, K, A_1, \ldots, A_l, \tilde{n}_p)$, *where* C *is the process executed by the candidates,* E *is the process executed by the examiners,* Q *is the process executed by the question committee,* K *is the process executed by the collector,* $A_1, \ldots, A_l$ *are the processes executed by the remaining authorities, and* $\tilde{n}_p$ *is the set of private channel names.*

Note that we make explicit the examiner E, the question committee Q, and the collector K among the authority processes although this is not strictly necessary. However, it turns out to be convenient for the formalisation of our security requirements.

All the principals playing the candidate role execute the same process C. However, each principal is instantiated with different variable values, e.g., keys, identities, and answers. Similarly, each principal playing any one of the authority role (e.g., examiner, question committee, collector, etc.) executes the respective processes with different values.

Definition 17 (Exam instance) *An* exam instance *of an exam protocol given by the tuple* $(C, A_1, \ldots, A_l, \tilde{n})$ *is a closed process*
$EP = \nu\tilde{n}.(C\sigma_{id_1}\sigma_{a_1} | \ldots | C\sigma_{id_j}\sigma_{a_j} | E\sigma_{id'_1}\sigma_{m_1} | \ldots | E\sigma_{id'_k}\sigma_{m_k} | Q\sigma_q | K\sigma_{test} | A_1 | \ldots | A_l)$, *where*

- $\tilde{n}$ *is the set of all restricted names, including the private channels;*

- $C\sigma_{id_i}\sigma_{a_i}$ *'s are the processes run by the candidates, where the substitutions* σ_{id_i} *and* σ_{a_i} *specify the identity and the answers associated with the* i^{th} *candidate;*

- $E\sigma_{id'_i}\sigma_{m_i}$ *'s are the processes run by the examiner authorities, where the substitution* $\sigma_{id'_i}$ *and* σ_{m_i} *specify the identity and the mark associated with the* i^{th} *examiner;*

- $Q\sigma_q$ *is the process run by the question committee authority, where the substitution σ_q specifies the exam questions;*

- $K\sigma_{test}$ *is the process run by the collector authority, where the substitution σ_{test} associates a test with an examiner for marking;*

- A_i *'s are the processes run by the remaining exam authorities.*

Definitions 16 and 17 capture the levels of detail and abstraction advocated in Chapter 2. The instance of an exam protocol can be customised by making processes A_i explicit. For example, the exam instance can be expanded with processes that model a mixnet for the generation of test pseudonyms (see Chapter 5), or a bulletin board that publishes the results of an exam (see Chapter 6).

As we shall see later, Definition 17 allows us to specify a considerable number of security requirements and is suitable for different types of exam protocols. Moreover, it equally supports either machine or human examiners as principals that mark answers.

Chapter 3

Security Requirements

This chapter identifies and specifies a number of authentication, privacy, and verifiability requirements. Those specifications form two formal frameworks for the security analysis of exam protocols. The specifications of authentication and privacy requirements are in the applied π-calculus and are based on definitions of *Exam protocol* (Definition 16) and *Exam instance* (Definition 17). The specifications of verifiability requirements are discussed in a more abstract model using a *set-theoretic* approach rather than a process algebra. Both approaches are useful for the analysis of different types of exams. As we shall see, this book takes advantage of both approaches to analyse traditional, computer-assisted, and Internet-based exam protocols.

The list of requirements presented in this chapter is not meant to be universal or exhaustive, although we find them highly desirable out of personal experience and discussions with colleagues. It means that certain exam protocols might demand additional requirements. However, we consider our set of requirements to be *fundamental* as similar requirements can be found in other independent works [Wei05, FOK+98], still only informally.

This chapter discusses verifiability as a mean to guarantee *transparency* in exams. While traditional exams can normally be observed through all the phases of the exam, computer-assisted exams may introduce opaqueness. In general, any operation performed by computers may not be observable, depending on the level of computer assistance. For example, computer markers may alter the evaluations of the tests, or malware in the collector may modify or drop the submitted tests. Thus, transparency demands *verifiable* exams. A verifiable exam can be checked for the presence or the absence of irregularities and provides evidence about fairness and correctness of marking. Moreover, verifiable exams foster public trust, as transparency can persuade the involved parties to comply with regulations.

Outline of the chapter. Section 3.1 examines different formal approaches for the specification of requirements and analysis of security protocols. Section 3.2 outlines the specification of authentication requirements, while Section 3.3 outlines privacy requirements. Section 3.4 contains the specification of 11 verifiability requirements for exams. Finally, Section 3.5 concludes the chapter.

© Springer International Publishing AG 2018
R. Giustolisi, *Modelling and Verification of Secure Exams*, Information Security
and Cryptography, https://doi.org/10.1007/978-3-319-67107-9_3

3.1   Formal Approaches

The key requirements at the heart of information security are authentication and privacy. More recently, the notion of verifiability has became central in democratic and meritocratic systems such as voting, auction, and exams. Those requirements have been studied in formal methods literature variously.

Authentication.   The notion of authentication has found different flavours in the literature. Gollmann [Gol96] argued that capturing the notion of authentication is difficult. Lowe [Low97] taxomised authentication in *Aliveness*, *Weak agreement*, *Non-injective agreement*, and *Injective agreement*. Despite the different interpretations, most of the approaches agree that authentication is a correspondence property: if the principal A accepts a message from B, then the principal B has actually sent that message to A. Typically, authentication can be captured by introducing *events* into the specification of protocol roles as seen at the end of Chapter 2. An event explicitly signals that a principal has completed part of a run of the protocol, and what data was used in that run. The placement of events into the protocol, the corresponding data, and the relationship between events can capture a precise authentication goal.

Privacy.   Several definitions for privacy have been proposed in the literature, such as secrecy, anonymity, unlinkability, and untraceability. Dolev and Yao [DY83] specified secrecy as a reachability property, meaning that a secret is not made available or disclosed to the attacker. Schneider and Sidiropoulos [SS96] formalised anonymity in CSP as the impossibility for an attacker to link a principal with a message. Deursen *et al.* [vDMR08] clarified that unlinkability considers whether links can be established between sender and receiver principals, while untraceability considers whether different communications can be attributed to the same principal. Ryan and Schneider [RS01] observed that the notion of non-interference [GM82] and bisimulation can be used to express security requirements. In this vein, several formal definitions of privacy have been proposed as equivalence-based properties. In the applied π-calculus, *observational equivalence* states that an observer cannot distinguish any difference between two processes, although they might perform different computations on different data.

Verifiability.   Another fundamental requirement of exams is verifiability. The notion of verifiability has been studied in domains close to exams, such as voting and auctions, and different models and requirements have been proposed since the beginning of 2010s [DHL13, KTV10, KRS10]. In voting, *individual verifiability* signifies that voters can verify that their votes have been handled correctly, namely "cast as intended", "recorded as cast", and "counted as recorded" [BT94, HS00]. The concept of *universal verifiability* has been introduced to express that auditors can verify the correctness of the tally using only public information [CF85, BT94, Ben87]. Kremer *et al.* [KRS10] formalised both individual and universal verifiability in the applied π-Calculus. They also introduced the requirement of *eligibility verifiability*, which expresses that auditors can verify that each vote in the election result was cast by a registered voter, and there is at most one vote per voter. Smyth *et al.* [SRKM10] used ProVerif to check verifiability in three voting protocols. They express the requirements as reachability properties. We also analyse exam protocols in ProVerif to validate our approaches. However, our model and definitions of verifiability are constrained neither to the applied π-Calculus nor to ProVerif. The sound and complete *verifiability-tests* that we use to specify our requirements are inspired by the work of Dreier *et al.* [DHL13], who formalised verifiability for e-auction.

Küsters *et al.* [KTV10] studied *accountability*. This requirement says that, in presence of a protocol failure, one can identify the principal responsible for the failure. The notion of accountability is strongly related to verifiability as the latter's goal is to check the presence of protocol failures. In their work, Küsters *et al.* give symbolic and computational definitions of verifiability, which they argue to be a weak variant of accountability. Differently from our approach, their framework has to be instantiated for each application by identifying relevant verifiability goals. In Chapter 6 we present a formalisation of accountability and a new exam protocol that ensures such requirement.

Guts *et al.* [GFZN09] defined *auditability* as the quality of a protocol, which stores a sufficient number of evidences, to convince an honest judge that specific properties are satisfied. As we shall see later, auditability expresses the same concept of universal verifiability as defined in this book: anyone, even an outsider without a private knowledge about the protocol execution, can verify that the system relies only on the available pieces of evidence.

Few papers list informally a few verifiability requirements. Castella-Roca *et al.* [CRHJDJ06] discuss a secure exam management system, and informally define authentication, privacy, correction and receipt fullness. Huszti and Pethő [HP10], whose protocol is analysed in Chapter 4, extend the requirements with secrecy and robustness. None of the works outlined above addresses verifiability.

Tools. There are several tools that support the automatic analysis of authentication, privacy, and verifiability. FDR [Ros97] is the most popular model checker for CSP, and contributed to the discovery of Lowe's attack. AVISPA [ABB+05] combines four techniques to analyse reachability properties (authentication and secrecy), and recently a security flaw in Google implementation of SAML 2.0 Single Sign-On Authentication was discovered [ACC+08] using that tool. ProVerif [Bla01] is an automatic protocol analyser that can prove reachability and equivalence-based properties. The input language of ProVerif is the applied π-calculus, which the tool automatically translates to Horn clauses. ProVerif proved to be one of the automatic analysers with the best performances [CLN09]. Moreover, it allows user-defined equational theories that extend security models with algebraic properties to weaken the perfect cryptography assumption. We thus choose to formalise our security requirements in the applied π-calculus and analyse the exam protocols with ProVerif.

Comparison with voting and auctions. Similar domains to exams, such as voting and auction, have seen significant advances as regards the study of security requirements. Beyond verifiability, formal definitions of privacy requirements have been proposed in the last years. Novel voting protocols [RS06, Adi08] have been formally analysed for a family of privacy requirements, such as ballot privacy, receipt-freeness, and coercion-resistance [DLL12, BHM08,

DKR09], while auction protocols have been analysed for privacy and fairness
requirements [DJP10, DLL13, DJL13].

It can be observed that only a few of security requirement definitions proposed in voting and auction domains are similar to ones we introduce for exams.
For example, answers originated by eligible candidates should be marked in an
exam. In the same way, only ballots cast by eligible voters should be recorded
in a voting system, and only offers submitted by eligible bidders should be
considered in an auction.

The requirement of mark privacy for exams is intuitively close to the definitions of ballot privacy for voting and losing bid privacy for auctions. However,
it can be noticed a subtle difference: voting usually requires ballot privacy also
towards the voting authority, while a mark eventually needs to be associated to
the candidate usually by means of an exam authority.

Other requirements have fundamental differences. In exams, the association
between an answer and its author should be preserved — even in the presence
of colluding candidates. Conversely, vote authorship is not a requirement for
voting, in fact unlinkability between voter and vote is a desired property. A
peculiar requirement for exam is to keep the questions secret until the testing
phase. In voting, the list of candidates is public, while in auctions the list of
goods is normally known to bidders. Moreover, exams may require anonymous
marking, namely answers are marked while ignoring their authors. This signifies
a sort of fixed-term anonymity since each mark eventually needs to be assigned
to the corresponding candidate.

3.2   Authentication

We begin the treatment of security requirements for exam with a set of five
authentication requirements specified in the applied π-calculus. This set is not
meant to be comprehensive, but it includes the basic authentication requirements that an exam protocol is normally expected to guarantee as corroborated
in the literature [Wei05, BGL13, FOK+98]. However, this set can be extended
with additional security requirements.

The authentication requirements capture the associations between the candidate's identity, the answer, and the mark being preserved through all the exam
phases. When authentication holds there is no loss, no injection, and in general
no manipulation of the exam tests from preparation to notification.

To model authentication requirements as correspondence properties, it is
necessary to define a number of relevant events. Events normally need to agree
with some arguments to capture authentication. Thus, we introduce the terms
that serve as arguments in our events as follows.

- id_c refers to the identity of the candidate;

- $ques$ denotes the question(s) of the test;

- ans denotes the answer of a test;

- $mark$ denotes the mark assigned to the test;

- id_e refers to the identity of the examiner;

- id_test refers to the identifier of the test.

The terms outlined above intuitively relates to the substitutions introduced in Definition 17. Their definitions are abstract enough to capture different exams. For example, the term id_test may coincide with the identity of the candidate if the exam requires no blind marking, or may be a pseudonym to if the exam requires anonymous marking.

We define a list of seven events that allow to specify five fundamental authentication requirements for exams. This list can be further extended to accommodate any additional requirements.

- **registered**$\langle id\_c \rangle$ means that the authority considers the candidate id_c registered for the exam. The event is inserted into the process of authority at the location where the registration of the candidate id_c concludes.

- **submitted**$\langle id\_c, ques, ans, id\_test \rangle$ means that the candidate id_c considers the test id_test, which consists of question $ques$ and answer ans, submitted for the exam. The event is inserted into the process of the candidate at the location where the test is sent to the collector.

- **collected**$\langle id\_c, ques, ans, id\_test \rangle$ means that the collector accepts the test id_test, which originates from the candidate id_c. The event is inserted into the process of the collector at the location where the test is considered as accepted.

- **distributed**$\langle id\_c, ques, ans, id\_test, id\_e \rangle$ means that the collector considers the test id_test, which originates from the candidate id_c, associated with the examiner id_e for marking. The event is inserted into the process of the collector at the location where the test is distributed to the examiner.

- **marked**$\langle ques, ans, mark, id\_test, id\_e \rangle$ means that the examiner id_e considers the test id_test, which consists of question $ques$ and answer ans, evaluated with $mark$. The event is inserted into the process of the examiner at the location where the test is marked.

- **stored**$\langle id\_c, id\_test, mark \rangle$ means that the authority considers the candidate id_c associated with $mark$. The event is inserted into the process of the authority at the location where it officially registers the mark assigned to the candidate.

- **notified**$\langle id\_c, id\_test \rangle mark$: means that the candidate id_c officially accepts the mark $mark$. The event is inserted into the process of the candidate at the location where the mark is considered accepted.

These events mark important steps of an exam protocol, and some can be associated with the phases of an exam. The event **registered** normally concludes the preparation phase, while **collected** concludes the testing phase. The event **distributed** begins the marking phase, which the event **marked** concludes. Finally, the event **notified** concludes the notification phase and the exam. Note that these events implicitly refer to the same exam session. However, one might want to parameterise all the events with a common term in order to distinguish among exam sessions.

The first authentication requirement we consider is *Candidate Authorisation*, which concerns preparation and testing. Informally, we want to capture the requirement that only registered candidates can take the exam. More specifically, the requirement says that if a candidate submits her test, then the candidate was correctly registered for the exam.

Definition 18 (Candidate Authorisation) *An exam protocol ensures* Candidate Authorisation *if for every exam process EP*

$$\texttt{submitted}\langle id\_c, ques, ans, id\_test \rangle \rightsquigarrow inj \texttt{registered}\langle id\_c \rangle$$

on every execution trace.

This requirement is modelled as injective correspondence assertion because the exam should consider only one submission per registered candidate.

The second authentication requirement that we advance is *Answer Authenticity*, which concerns the testing phase. It states that the collector should consider only answers that candidates actually submitted, and that the contents of each collected test are not modified after submission. It says that a test must be bound to a candidate identity. A way to enforce this would be to only give a test to a candidate after she inserts in the test the same details that authenticated her. This candidate becomes the test assignee. With exams that are not computer assisted, for example, an authority can check that the candidate writes down the right details on the test, or the authority can write them down personally. The requirement implies that two candidates will be unable to get tested on each other's questions, something that could be desirable if they found their respective questions too difficult. Moreover, it should be considered only one test from each candidate, namely every time the collector process emits **collected**, there is a distinct earlier occurrence of the event **submitted** that satisfies the relationship between their arguments. This is enforced by the injective formula below.

Definition 19 (Answer Authenticity) *An exam protocol ensures* Answer Authenticity *if for every exam process EP*

$$\texttt{collected}\langle id\_c, ques, ans, id\_test \rangle \rightsquigarrow inj \texttt{submitted}\langle id\_c, ques, ans, id\_test \rangle$$

on every execution trace.

The third requirement is *Test Origin Authentication* and concerns preparation and testing. Informally, it says that the collector should accept only tests that originate from registered candidates. This requirement should be modelled as an injective agreement to enforce that only one test from each registered candidate is actually collected.

Definition 20 (Test Origin Authentication) *An exam protocol ensures* Test Origin Authentication *if for every exam process EP*

$$\texttt{collected}\langle id\_c, ques, ans, id\_test \rangle \rightsquigarrow inj \texttt{registered}\langle id\_c \rangle$$

on every execution trace.

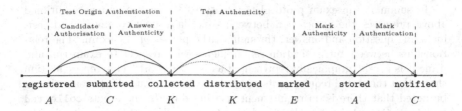

Figure 3.1: A graphical representation of the authentication requirements for exams

Another authentication requirement is *Test Authenticity* and concerns testing and marking. Since the collector distributes the tests possibly among different examiners, Test Authenticity insists that the examiner only marks the tests intended for him. Moreover, the contents of each test should not be modified until after the tests are marked by the examiner. This requirement can be modelled as injective agreement.

Definition 21 (Test Authenticity) *An exam protocol ensures* Test Authenticity *if for every exam process EP*

$$\texttt{marked}\langle ques, ans, mark, id\_test, id\_e \rangle \rightsquigarrow$$
$$inj\texttt{collected}\langle id\_c, ques, ans, id\_test \rangle \cup$$
$$inj\texttt{distributed}\langle id\_c, ques, ans, id\_test, id\_e \rangle$$

on every execution trace.

The requirement *Mark Authenticity* concerns marking and notification. It prescribes that a mark should be correctly recorded for the corresponding test and candidate, namely that the administrator should store the mark assigned to a test during marking by the examiner. This contributes to a finer and fuller coverage of all the phases of an exam in terms of authentication, as Figure 3.1 will confirm graphically.

Definition 22 (Mark Authenticity) *An exam protocol ensures* Mark Authenticity *if for every exam process EP*

$$\texttt{stored}\langle id\_c, id\_test \rangle mark \rightsquigarrow \texttt{marked}\langle ques, ans, mark, id\_test, id\_e \rangle$$

on every execution trace.

A final, important requirement is *Mark Authentication*, which says that the candidate is notified with the same mark that has been stored by the authority.

Definition 23 (Mark Authentication) *An exam protocol ensures* Mark Authentication *if for every exam process EP*

$$\texttt{notified}\langle id\_c, id\_test \rangle mark \rightsquigarrow \texttt{stored}\langle id\_c, id\_test \rangle mark$$

on every execution trace.

In summary, an exam protocol that ensures all the requirements outlined above preserves the association between candidate identity, mark, and test, including question and answer, through all the phases of the exam. The relationships between authentication requirements with respect to exam run and principals can be graphically represented as in Figure 3.1. This representation shows that the stated requirements rest on an ordered sequence of events. It can be noted that there is no requirement relating directly the events collected and distributed (i.e., the densely dotted arrows). We chose not to specify the requirement *"the collector distributes the accepted tests"* since such requirement is usually enforced by the sequential execution of the collector process as both events belong to the same process. Moreover, it always holds if the common arguments of the two events are derived from the same source, for example, if the common arguments are built from the same message input. In general, this and other requirements get more interesting if events reflect tasks that are executed by different roles, according to the levels of detail and abstraction of the exam protocol. Hence, an exam protocol that specifies a huge number of tasks, might allow to express more events thus novel authentication requirements.

Figure 3.1 also emphasises that the combination of these requirements produce novel requirements. If an exam protocol guarantees Candidate Authorisation and Answer Authenticity, then the protocol also guarantees Test Origin Authentication, namely the tests submitted by registered candidates are actually collected. Conversely, a protocol that guarantees Test Origin Authentication may guarantee neither Candidate Authorisation nor Answer Authenticity. Test Origin Authentication only states that collected tests originate from registered candidates without considering the actually submitted tests. It follows that a test modified after submission may meet Test Origin Authentication but not Answer Authenticity.

In general, if we consider a requirement in a certain phase of the exam, we cannot infer anything about other phases. For example, Mark Authenticity signifies that the administrator stores the same mark that the examiner assigned to the candidate's test. However, the test provided by the invigilator to the examiner may contain a different answer with respect to the answer the candidate submitted at testing. Only if the exam protocol also guarantees Answer Authenticity and Test Authenticity are the contents of the tests identical through the whole exam.

3.3   Privacy

The five privacy requirements described in this section aim to capture secrecy of marks and anonymity of tests and examiners.

To model privacy requirements as equivalence properties, we use the definition of labelled bisimilarity ($\approx_l$), which was defined in Section 2.7.

We introduce two notations to make clear the requirements. First, we denote with "$EP_I[\_]$" the context of the process EP pruned of identities that appear in the set I. For example, the process $\nu\tilde{n}.(\_|\_|\ C\sigma_{id_3}\sigma_{a_3}|\dots|C\sigma_{id_j}\sigma_{a_j}|\ E\sigma_{id_1'}\sigma_{m_1}|\dots\ |E\sigma_{id_k'}\sigma_{m_k}|Q\sigma_q|K\sigma_{dist}|A_1|\dots|A_l)$ can be concisely written as $EP_{\{id_1,id_2\}}[\_]$. Such compact notation is useful to specify and focus exactly on the processes concerned by the requirement. For example, we can write $EP_{\{id_1,id_2\}}[C\sigma_{id_1}\sigma_{a_1}|C\sigma_{id_2}\sigma_{a_2}]$ to reason about candidates id_1 and id_2 without repeating the entire exam instance.

Second, we denote with "$EP|_e$" the process EP pruned of the code that follows the event e. For example, the process $EP|_{\texttt{marked}}$ considers an exam instance that terminates at marking, namely after the event **marked** is emitted. This notation is useful to capture fixed-term requirements such as anonymous marking, which is intended to hold until after the marking, but is eventually falsified at notification when the mark is assigned to the candidate.

The first privacy requirement we consider is *Question Indistinguishability*. This requirement says that the questions are not revealed until the testing phase begins. Thus, it is a fixed-term requirement that sees the exam process ending with the preparation phase.

Definition 24 (Question Indistinguishability) *An exam protocol ensures* Question Indistinguishability *if for any exam process EP and any questions q_1 and q_2*

$$EP[Q\sigma_{q_1}]|_{\texttt{registered}} \approx_l EP[Q\sigma_{q_2}]|_{\texttt{registered}}$$

Question Indistinguishability states that two processes with different questions have to be observationally equivalent until after the preparation phase. Note that this requirement is more stringent than reachability-based secrecy because the attacker should not be able to distinguish whether the exam will use q_1 or q_2 despite he knows both the questions in advance. For instance, the attacker cannot say whether the questions of the current exam are similar to the questions of the previous exam, which are on attacker's knowledge. The analysis of Question Indistinguishability requires the question committee to be honest otherwise they could reveal the questions to the attacker making the requirement useless. However, this analysis is particularly interesting when considering corrupted candidates who may want to know the questions in advance. For example, in the particular case of a corrupted candidate e id_1, the requirement gets rewritten as outlined below, where honest candidates are replaced with corrupted ones using the definition of corrupted process defined in Section 2.7.

$$EP_{\{id_1\}}[(C\sigma_{id_1}\sigma_{a_1})^{c_1,c_2}|A\sigma_{q_1}]|_{\texttt{registered}} \approx_l$$
$$EP_{\{id_1\}}[(C\sigma_{id_1}\sigma_{a_1})^{c_1,c_2}|A\sigma_{q_2}]|_{\texttt{registered}}$$

The next requirement is *Anonymous Marking*, which covers preparation, testing, and marking. This requirement signifies that the examiner marks a test while ignoring its author, namely an anonymous test. It is a clear contribution to the fairness of the marking. As it stands, the requirement insists on anonymity only until the point that the examiner affixes a mark. Anonymous Marking can be specified as two exam instances in which the processes of two candidates who swap their answers cannot be distinguished until after the end of the marking phase.

Definition 25 (Anonymous Marking) *An exam protocol ensures* Anonymous Marking *if any exam process EP, any two candidates id_1 and id_2, and any two answers a_1 and a_2*

$$EP_{\{id_1,id_2\}}[C\sigma_{id_1}\sigma_{a_1}|C\sigma_{id_2}\sigma_{a_2}]|_{\texttt{marked}} \approx_l EP_{\{id_1,id_2\}}[C\sigma_{id_1}\sigma_{a_2}|C\sigma_{id_2}\sigma_{a_1}]|_{\texttt{marked}}$$

In other words, Anonymous Marking says that the process where candidate id_1 submits a_1 and candidate id_2 submits a_2 is indistinguishable to the process where candidate id_1 submits a_2 and candidate id_2 submits a_1. It prevents the attacker to obtain the identity of the candidate who submits a certain answer before the marking ends.

Similarly to Question Indistinguishability, it is interesting to consider corrupted principals in the analysis of Anonymous Marking, which means that nobody knows who submitted a test while this is being marked, except the official author of the test. An implication is that test anonymity during marking will even resist collusion of the examiner with other authorities and candidates. Again, the definition of corrupted process can model corrupted examiners and authorities. The definition can be also used to specify corrupted candidates, however the candidates id_1 and id_2 who submit two different answers have to be honest. This avoids the corner case in which all candidates but one reveal their answers to the attacker, who can easily associate the remaining answer with the honest candidate and thus trivially violate the requirement.

We now consider the requirement of *Anonymous Examiner*, which concerns all the phases of an exam. It concerns all the phases of an exam because examiner anonymity could be required to hold forever to prevent bribing or coercion. Thus, the requirement of Anonymous Examiner says that no candidate knows which examiner marked her test. This requirement can be formalised as:

Definition 26 (Anonymous Examiner) *An exam protocol ensures* Anonymous Examiner *if for any exam process EP, any two candidates id_1 and id_2, any two examiners id_1' and id_2', any two marks m_1 and m_2, and two associations $test_1$ and $test_2$*

$$EP_{\{id_1,id_2,id_1',id_2'\}} \; [C\sigma_{id_1}\sigma_{a_1}|C\sigma_{id_2}\sigma_{a_2}|E\sigma_{id_1'}\sigma_{m_1}|E\sigma_{id_2'}\sigma_{m_2}|K\sigma_{test_1}] \approx_l$$

$$EP_{\{id_1,id_2,id_1',id_2'\}} \; [C\sigma_{id_1}\sigma_{a_1}|C\sigma_{id_2}\sigma_{a_2}|E\sigma_{id_1'}\sigma_{m_2}|E\sigma_{id_2'}\sigma_{m_1}|K\sigma_{test_2}]$$

where

- *σ_{test_1} associates the test of candidate id_1 to examiner id_1' and the test of candidate id_2 to examiner id_2';*

- *σ_{test_2} associates the test of candidate id_1 to examiner id_2' and the test of candidate id_2 to examiner id_1'.*

Thus, Anonymous Examiner states that a process in which the examiner id_1' evaluates the test of candidate id_1 while the examiner id_2' evaluates the test of candidate id_2 is indistinguishable to the process in which the examiner id_1' evaluates the test of candidate id_2 while the examiner id_2' evaluates the test of candidate id_1. Note that the two marks σ_{m_1} and σ_{m_2} are swapped on examiner processes to ensure that each test is evaluated with the same mark in both cases. In the field of peer review systems, this requirement is known as *blind review*. The requirement of *double-bind review* instead refers to a peer review system that ensure both Anonymous Examiner and Anonymous Marking, namely anonymity is provided to both authors and examiners. However, peer review systems usually assume that the collector knows which examiner evaluates a test, while other systems may not. To ensure a stronger version of Anonymous Marking it is possible to model corrupted collectors, candidates, and any other principal, provided that examiners id'_1 and id'_2 are honest. This would avoid the corner case in which an examiner reveals the mark to the attacker, a case that would trivially violate the requirement.

The requirement of *Mark Privacy* concerns all phases of an exam. It states that the mark ultimately attributed to a candidate is treated as valuable personal information of the candidates. More specifically, no one learns the marks, besides the examiner, the concerned candidate, and the authority responsible for the notification. This means that the marks cannot be public.

Definition 27 (Mark Privacy) *An exam protocol ensures* Mark Privacy *if for any exam process EP and any two marks m_1 and m_2*

$$EP_{\{id'\}}[E\sigma_{id'}\sigma_{m_1}] \approx_l EP_{\{id'\}}[E\;\sigma_{id'}\sigma_{m_2}].$$

The definition of Mark Privacy means that a process in which the examiner id' assigns the mark m_1 to an answer cannot be distinguished from a process in which the same examiner assigns a different mark m_2 to the same answer. This is a strict requirement because an exam protocol that guarantees Mark Privacy cannot publicly disclose the marks even if these cannot be associated with the corresponding candidates. In fact, the publication of the marks allows the attacker to distinguish the processes. Again, it can be assumed that some candidates and examiners are corrupted, namely collaborate with the attacker to find out the marks of other candidates. However, the examiner who assigns the different marks, the two candidates who submit the tests, and the authority in charge of the notification of the marks should be honest. Otherwise, any of these could violate the requirement by revealing the mark to the attacker.

Since Mark Privacy can be a requirement too strong to satisfy, we introduce a variant called *Mark Anonymity*. This requirement states that no one learns the association between a mark and the corresponding candidate. Intuitively, an exam protocol that publishes the list of all marks might still ensure Mark Anonymity, but not Mark Privacy. This is a common privacy requirement in scenarios like public competitions, in which marks are published and associated with a list of pseudonyms for transparency. Mark Anonymity can be defined as follows:

Definition 28 (Mark Anonymity) *An exam protocol ensures* Mark Anonymity *if for any exam process EP, any two candidates id_1, id_2, any examiners id', any two answers a_1, a_2, two substitutions σ_{m_a} and σ_{m_b} and an association test*

$$EP_{\{id_1,id_2,id'\}}[C\sigma_{id_1}\sigma_{a_1}|C\sigma_{id_2}\sigma_{a_2}|E\sigma_{id'}\sigma_{m_a}|K\sigma_{test}] \approx_l$$
$$EP_{\{id_1,id_2,id'\}}[C\sigma_{id_1}\sigma_{a_1}|C\sigma_{id_2}\sigma_{a_2}|E\sigma_{id'}\sigma_{m_b}|K\sigma_{test}]$$

where

- σ_{test} *associates the tests of both candidates id_1 and id_2 to the examiner id';*

- σ_{m_a} *attributes the mark m_1 to the answer a_1 and the mark m_2 to the answer a_2;*

- σ_{m_b} *attributes the mark m_2 to the answer a_1 and the mark m_1 to the answer a_2.*

In other words, a process in which an examiner evaluates two answers a_1 and a_2 respectively with m_1 and m_2 is indistinguishable for the attacker with a process in which the examiner evaluates the same answers but with swapped marks, namely the examiner marks a_1 and a_2 respectively with m_2 and m_1. In doing so, the authority can make the list of marks public assuming the attacker cannot associate the marks to the candidates. The analysis of Mark Anonymity requires the two concerned candidates, the examiner, and the notifier authority to be honest. Otherwise, they can simply reveal the answer and the associated mark to allow the attacker to distinguish the two case processes. Other principals can be considered corrupted. It can be noted that an exam protocol that guarantees *Mark Privacy* also guarantees *Mark Anonymity*. In fact, σ_{m_a} and σ_{m_b} defined in Mark Anonymity are special instances of σ_{m_1} and σ_{m_2} defined in Mark Privacy.

3.4   Verifiability

In this section, we discuss a set of eleven verifiability requirements for exam protocols and introduce a methodology for their formal analysis. In general, a protocol is verifiable with respect to a specific property if a *verifiability-test* exists, namely an algorithm that decides the property, and the algorithm is sound and complete.

New framework. Differently from the framework advanced earlier in this chapter, we propose a formal framework based on multisets that abstract away from the applied π-calculus constraints and is suitable for both symbolic and computational analysis. In Chapter 2, we observed that any exam involves at least the candidate role plus other possible authority roles, and that the run of an exam can be represented as the sequential execution of preparation, testing, marking, and notification phases. From these observations, we build the framework for the analysis of verifiability. Earlier in this chapter we advanced a framework based on the applied π-calculus, hence supported by an operational semantics. Here the framework for verifiability comes without such semantics. On the one hand, a more abstract framework requires to map the model onto one that allows the analysis of the protocol. On the other hand, it allows for a wider choice of analysis methods, regardless whether they are based on the symbolic or computational model. In Chapter 5 we validate this framework by analysing verifiability in a novel exam protocol, using ProVerif as analysis method.

We view the abstract model of an exam consisting of four sets, three relations, and one function. The four sets are of candidate's identities I, questions Q, answers A, and marks M. The three relations Accepted, Marked, and Assigned, link candidates, questions, answers, and marks along the four phases. A test consists of the pair $(Q \times A)$ of questions and answers. The function Correct maps a mark to a test. It is assumed that sets and relations are built from data logs such as registers or repositories.

Definition 29 (Exam (abstract model))

An exam E is a tuple (I, Q, A, M, α) where I of type $\mathcal{I}$ is a set of candidate identities, Q of type $\mathcal{Q}$ is a set of questions, A of type $\mathcal{A}$ is a set of answers, M

of type $\mathcal{M}$ *is a set of marks, and* α *is the set of the following relations:*

- `Accepted` $\subseteq I \times (Q \times A)$: *the candidates' tests accepted by the collector authority;*

- `Marked` $\subseteq I \times (Q \times A) \times M$: *the marks given to the candidates' tests;*

- `Assigned` $\subseteq I \times M$: *the marks assigned to the candidates;*

- `Correct` $: (Q \times A) \to \mathcal{M}$: *the function used to mark a test.*

Definition 29 can be extended with two specific subsets:

- $I_r \subseteq I$ as the set of identities of candidates who registered for the exam;

- $Q_g \subseteq Q$ as the set of questions generated by the question committee.

It can be noted that this approach can model exam executed either honestly or with frauds. For example, the set $I \setminus I_r$ contains the identities of the unregistered candidates who took the exam. Similarly, the set $Q \setminus Q_g$ contains the illegitimate questions administered at the exam. An honest execution of an exam requires $(I \setminus I_r) = (Q \setminus Q_g) = \emptyset$.

The function `Correct` models any objective mapping that assigns a mark to an answer. This works well for multiple-choice tests, but it is inappropriate for short answer and essay tests. The evaluation of a short answer or essay is hardly objective: the ambiguities of natural language can lead to subjective interpretations by the examiner. In this case, it is not possible to verify the correctness of the marking, whatever model is considered. In other words, an exam protocol that does not allow a definition of the function `Correct` cannot be checked for the correctness of the marking.

Verifiability requirements. A verifiability requirement has the form $t(e) \Leftrightarrow c$, where the verifiability-test $t(e)$ is a function from $\mathcal{E} \to$ `bool`, where $\mathcal{E}$ is the set of data e, and c is a predicate that models the specific property. The data needed to run the verifiability-test are obtained from the available information about the execution of the exam and from the private knowledge of the involved roles. It is assumed that the pieces of data become available after the exam concludes and are not subject to further changes.

To be verifiable an exam should be *testable*, namely it should provide an algorithm (the verifiability-test) that checks a specific property on the exam execution. Specifically, we refer to the existence of an algorithm that takes in some data and outputs true or false. Such algorithm may be either explicitly provided by the protocol designer or found by the protocol analyst. The following definition resumes the notion of testable exam.

Definition 30 (Testable exam) *An exam protocol is* testable *if it provides a verifiable-test that checks a desired property.*

Being testable is not a sufficient condition for an exam to be verifiable because the verifiability-test should be sound and complete ($\Leftrightarrow$) for the specific property: the success of the verifiability-test is a *sufficient* condition for c to hold (soundness $\Rightarrow$), and the success of the verifiability-test is a *necessary* condition for c to hold (completeness $\Leftarrow$). This is captured by the definition of *verifiable exam.*

Requirement	Individual Verifiability	Universal Verifiability
Registration		$R_{UV}(e) \Leftrightarrow$ $I_r \supseteq \{i : (i,x) \in \text{Accepted}\}$
Question Validity	$QV_{IV}(i,q,a,m,p) \Leftrightarrow (q \in Q_g)$	
Marking Correctness	$MC_{IV}(i,q,a,m,p) \Leftrightarrow$ $(\text{Correct}(q,a) = m)$	$MC_{UV}(e) \Leftrightarrow$ $(\forall(i,x,m) \in \text{Marked},$ $\text{Correct}(x) = m$
Test Integrity	$ETI_{IV}(i,q,a,m,p) \Leftrightarrow$ $((i,(q,a)) \in \text{Accepted}$ $\wedge \exists m' : (i,(q,a),m') \in \text{Marked})$	$ETI_{UV}(e) \Leftrightarrow \text{Accepted} =$ $\{(i,x) : (i,x,m) \in \text{Marked}\}$
Test Markedness	$ETM_{IV}(i,q,a,m,p) \Leftrightarrow$ $(\exists m' : (i,(q,a),m') \in \text{Marked}))$	$ETM_{UV}(e) \Leftrightarrow \text{Accepted} \supseteq$ $\{(i,x) : (i,x,m) \in \text{Marked}\}$
Marking Integrity	$MI_{IV}(i,q,a,m,p) \Leftrightarrow$ $\exists m' : ((i,(q,a),m') \in \text{Marked}$ $\wedge(i,m') \in \text{Assigned})$	$MI_{UV}(e) \Leftrightarrow \text{Assigned} =$ $\{(i,m) : (i,x,m) \in \text{Marked}\}$
Marking Notification Integrity	$MNI_{IV}(i,q,a,m,p) \Leftrightarrow$ $(i,m) \in \text{Assigned}$	

Table 3.1: Individual and universal verifiability

Definition 31 (Verifiable exam) *An exam protocol is* verifiable *for a desired property if the exam is testable and the corresponding verifiable-test is* sound *and* complete.

With a security take, a verifiability-test should be sound in presence of an attacker and corrupted principals. It means that when the test succeeds the property holds despite the presence of attacker and corrupted principals. The verifiability-test should be complete to avoid trivialities: a verifiability-test that always returns false is sound but useless.

Sound verifiability-tests cannot be complete if a corrupted principal is allowed to submit incorrect data, since the verifiability-test would fail although the property holds. Thus, a verifiability-test should be complete in the sense that if all principals follow the protocol, then the verifiability-test must succeed.

A verifiability-test can be run by exam principals or outsiders, a distinction that leads to two notions of verifiability requirements: *individual* and *universal*. In the scenario of exam, we view individual verifiability as verifiability from the perspective of the candidate role. The candidate can feed the verifiability-test with the private knowledge acquired during the exam, namely the candidate's identity, the test, the mark, and the messages the candidate exchanged with the other principals through the exam.

We view universal verifiability as verifiability from the perspective of an external auditor or outsider. This role can be played by auditors who acquire no private knowledge during the exam. The auditor typically has no tasks associated to an exam, thus he has no candidate's identity, he has not seen the exam's questions, answered any of them, and he did not receive any mark. Besides, he has not interacted with any of the exam principals. In short, the auditor runs the verifiability-tests only using the exam's available pieces of data.

The list of proposed verifiability requirements is not meant to be exhaustive but aims to cover all the phases of an exam. The requirements concern the verifiability of candidate registration, the validity of questions, and the integrity of tests, marks, and notification. In the remainder of the section we detail the requirements, which are concisely listed in Table 3.1. Generally speaking, an exam is fully verifiable, if it ensures all the verifiability requirements.

3.4.1   Individual Verifiability

Individual verifiability allows the candidate to verify some aspects of the exam using the public data that is available from the execution of the exam plus the candidate's private knowledge. The candidate knows her identity i, the test she submitted, which consists of question q and answer a, and the notified mark m. The candidate also knows the perspective p of the run of the exam. The perspective consists of the messages the candidate sent and received during the run of the exam. Thus, the data is a tuple (i, q, a, m, p). Note that the candidate's perspective p is not necessary to specify the predicate that models the properties to verify. In fact, the perspective never appears in the predicate c. However, the perspective may be necessary to implement the verifiability-test $t(e)$.

The six individual verifiability requirements concern the validity of the questions, the integrity of the submitted test, and the correctness and integrity of the mark notified to the candidate.

The first requirement is *Question Validity*, which signifies that the candidate can check that she received the questions actually generated by the question committee. The requirement is modelled by a verifiability-test that returns true if the questions q received by the candidate belong to the set of the valid questions Q_g generated by the question committee. This is formalised as follows:

Definition 32 (Question Validity I.V.) *Given an exam E and a set of verifiability-tests β, then (E, β) is* question validity verifiable *if there is a verifiability-test* $\mathtt{QV_{IV}} : \mathcal{E} \to \mathtt{bool}$ *in β such that*

$$\mathtt{QV_{IV}}(i, q, a, m, p) \Leftrightarrow (q \in Q_g)$$

The next requirement is *Marking Correctness*, which says that the candidate can verify that the mark she received is correctly computed on her test. It can be formalised as:

Definition 33 (Marking Correctness I.V.) *Given an exam E and a set of verifiability-tests β, then (E, β) is* marking correctness verifiable *if there is a verifiability-test* $\mathtt{MC_{IV}} : \mathcal{E} \to \mathtt{bool}$ *in β such that*

$$\mathtt{MC_{IV}}(i, q, a, m, p) \Leftrightarrow (\mathtt{Correct}(q, a) = m)$$

A way to ensure Marking Correctness is to give the candidate access to the marking algorithm, so she can compute again the mark and compare it with the one she received. As we discussed in Section 3.4, this makes perfect sense with multiple-choice tests, but it makes not in the case of short answers and survey tests. However, one can envisage other ways to convince the candidate she received the correct mark, provided the examiner follows the marking algorithm correctly. For example, the candidate could check that the integrity of her test is preserved from submission until marking, and that the integrity of the mark is preserved from marking until notification. The remaining individual verifiability requirements cover these very checks.

The third requirement is *Test Integrity*, which states that the candidate can check that her test is accepted and marked as she submitted it. It is formalised as follows:

Definition 34 (Test Integrity I.V.) *Given an exam E and a set of verifiability-tests β, then (E, β) is* test integrity verifiable *if there is a verifiability-test* $\text{ETI}_{\text{IV}} : \mathcal{E} \to \text{bool}$ *in β such that*

$$\text{ETI}_{\text{IV}}(i, q, a, m, p) \Leftrightarrow \big((i, (q, a)) \in \text{Accepted} \land \exists m' : (i, (q, a), m') \in \text{Marked}\big)$$

Since the verifiability-tests are run after the conclusion of the exam, Test Integrity cannot capture the scenario in which a test is modified before the marking and put back to its original version after marking. Such scenario can be detected by verifying Marking Correctness.

Another requirement that concerns the integrity of the test is *Test Markedness*, which says that the candidate can check that the test she submitted is marked without modification. It can be specified as follows:

Definition 35 (Test Markedness I.V.) *Given an exam E and a set of verifiability-tests β, then (E, β) is* test markedness verifiable *if there is a verifiability-test* $\text{ETM}_{\text{IV}} : \mathcal{E} \to \text{bool}$ *in β such that*

$$\text{ETM}_{\text{IV}}(i, q, a, m, p) \Leftrightarrow (\exists m' : (i, (q, a), m') \in \text{Marked})$$

Note that the predicate of Test Markedness coincides with the one of Test Integrity pruned of "$(i, (q, a)) \in \text{Accepted}$". Thus, if ETI_{IV} succeeds, then ETM_{IV} also succeeds, namely $\text{ETI}_{\text{IV}}(i, q, a, m, p) \Rightarrow \text{ETM}_{\text{IV}}(i, q, a, m, p)$. However, if the ETI_{IV} fails, but ETM_{IV} succeeds, it follows that the test of the candidate is modified upon acceptance but put back to its original version before marking. This may be not a security issue for the candidate since her test is marked as submitted. However, the candidate can report this issue to the responsible authority for further investigation. Another scenario where an exam protocol may provide ETM_{IV} but not ETI_{IV} is when there is a lack of available data at the conclusion of the exam.

The next requirement is *Mark Integrity*, which signifies that the candidate can verify that the mark attributed to her test is assigned to her without any modification. This requirement is formalised as follows:

Definition 36 (Mark Integrity I.V.) *Given an exam E and a set of verifiability-tests β, then (E, β) is* mark integrity verifiable *if there is a verifiability-test* $\text{MI}_{\text{IV}} : \mathcal{E} \to \text{bool}$ *in β such that*

$$\text{MI}_{\text{IV}}(i, q, a, m, p) \Leftrightarrow \exists m' : \big((i, (q, a), m') \in \text{Marked} \land (i, m') \in \text{Assigned}\big)$$

The last requirement is *Mark Notification Integrity*, which says that the candidate can check she received the mark assigned to her. This requirement is formalised as:

Definition 37 (Mark Notification Integrity I.V.) *Given an exam E and a set of verifiability-tests β, then (E, β) is* mark notification integrity verifiable *if there is a verifiability-test* $\text{MNI}_{\text{IV}} : \mathcal{E} \to \text{bool}$ *in β such that*

$$\text{MNI}_{\text{IV}}(i, q, a, m, p) \Leftrightarrow (i, m) \in \text{Assigned}$$

There is a subtle difference between the two last definitions. MI_{IV} can succeed despite the candidate is notified with a mark that is different from the one assigned to her, while MNI_{IV} cannot. Conversely, if MNI_{IV} succeeds, then MI_{IV} could fail if the examiner evaluated the test with a different mark.

3.4.2 Universal Verifiability

The definitions of universal verifiability are not pivoted around any exam role, but consider the viewpoint of an external auditor. The auditor runs the verifiability tests on the public data available after an exam protocol run. Hence, the knowledge of the auditor consists of a general variable e that contains the data.

The five universal verifiability requirements concern the registration of the candidates and the integrity of the batch of tests from the submission until after the marking. The requirements of Question Validity and of Mark Notification Integrity, which are definitions relevant for individual verifiability, are hard to capture in the context of universal verifiability. This is because the external auditor has no knowledge of the questions nor of the marks received by the candidates, but only of public data.

The first universal verifiability requirement we consider is *Registration*, which says that an auditor can check that all accepted tests are submitted by registered candidates. Thus, the collector should have considered only tests that originated from eligible candidates. This requirement can be specified as:

Definition 38 (Registration U.V.) *Given an exam E and a set of verifiability-tests β, then (E, β) is* registration verifiable *if there is a verifiability-test* $\mathsf{R_{UV}} : \mathcal{E} \to \mathtt{bool}$ *in β such that*

$$\mathsf{R_{UV}}(e) \Leftrightarrow I_r \supseteq \{i : (i, x) \in \mathtt{Accepted}\}$$

Note that the superset symbol is preferred over strict equality since a candidate may register for an exam but may not show at testing. Thus, the collector may accept fewer tests than registered candidates.

The next requirement is *Marking Correctness*, which signifies that an auditor can check that all the marks attributed by the examiners to the tests are computed correctly. It is formalised as follows:

Definition 39 (Marking Correctness U.V.) *Given an exam E and a set of verifiability-tests β, then (E, β) is* marking correctness universally verifiable *if there is a verifiability-test* $\mathsf{MC_{UV}} : \mathcal{E} \to \mathtt{bool}$ *in β such that*

$$(\mathsf{MC_{UV}}(e)) \Leftrightarrow (\forall (i, x, m) \in \mathtt{Marked}, \ \mathtt{Correct}(x) = m))$$

Marking Correctness makes the same arguments about free-response of tests we observed for Marking Correctness. However, for the sake of transparency, it can be assumed that exam authorities allow auditors to access the logs of the exam such that the auditors can inspect the marking process.

The third requirement is *Test Integrity*, which says that an auditor can verify that all and only accepted tests are marked without any modification. It means that the auditor can be convinced that no test is modified, added, or deleted until the end of marking. This requirement is formalised as:

Definition 40 (Test Integrity U.V.) *Given an exam E and a set of verifiability-tests β, then (E, β) is* test integrity universally verifiable *if there is a verifiability-test* $\mathsf{ETI_{UV}} : \mathcal{E} \to \mathtt{bool}$ *in β such that*

$$(\mathsf{ETI_{UV}}(e)) \Leftrightarrow (\mathtt{Accepted} = \{(i, x) : (i, x, m) \in \mathtt{Marked}\})$$

The equality symbol in the predicate specification enforces that at marking no test has been added or removed from the batch of accepted tests.

The next requirement is *Test Markedness*, which says that an auditor can check that only the accepted tests are marked without modification. It is formalised as follows:

Definition 41 (Test Markedness U.V.) *Given an exam E and a set of verifiability-tests β, then (E, β) is* test markedness universally verifiable *if there exists a verifiability-test* $\text{ETM}_{UV} : \mathcal{E} \to \text{bool}$ *in β such that*

$$(\text{ETM}_{UV}(e)) \Leftrightarrow (\text{Accepted} \supseteq \{(i, x) : (i, x, m) \in \text{Marked}\})$$

It can be noted that Test Markedness is a relaxed version of Test Integrity because the predicate of the former definition does not require strict equality of the two multisets. Thus, if ETI_{UV} fails but ETM_{UV} succeeds, it follows that at least one accepted test has not been marked. This scenario however may not be a security problem. For example, the rules of the exam may allow the candidate to drop the examination after testing. Conversely, the scenario in which an examiner marks a test that was not accepted is normally considered a violation of the exam.

The last requirement we consider is Mark Integrity, which signifies that an auditor can check that all and only the marks associated to the tests are assigned to the corresponding candidates with no modifications. This is formalised as:

Definition 42 (Mark Integrity U.V.) *Given an exam E and a set of verifiability-tests β, then (E, β) is* mark integrity universally verifiable *if there exists a verifiability-test* $\text{MI}_{UV} : \mathcal{E} \to \text{bool}$ *in β such that*

$$(\text{MI}_{UV}(e)) \Leftrightarrow (\text{Assigned} = \{(i, m) : (i, x, m) \in \text{Marked}\})$$

The equality symbol in the specification of the predicate enforces that no pair of candidates and marks have been added or removed from the batch of marked tests.

To conclude, it can be observed that the combination of registration, test integrity, and mark integrity universal verifiability enforces the verifiability from preparation to notification of an exam protocol.

3.5 Conclusion

This chapter discusses two formal frameworks for the security analysis of exam protocols. The first framework permits the definition of six authentication and five privacy requirements for exams, counting a total of eleven fundamental requirements. The framework takes advantage of the applied π-calculus and allows the analysis of exams in the symbolic model. The use of process algebras is a well-known approach to rigorously model authentication and privacy of security systems, notably for voting and auction systems. However, such approaches have some limitations that are lifted up in the approach adopted to formulate verifiability for exams.

The second framework advanced in this chapter allows us to define verifiability requirements. The domain of exam has unique features that call for verifiability definitions that are different from those proposed for voting and auctions. The eleven requirements, which are classified in individual and universal verifiability categories, are specified in a formal and abstract model that opens up opportunities for both symbolic and computational analysis. This model contrasts the frameworks proposed for the verifiability of voting and auction protocols, as the latter usually focus on cryptographic protocols. Intuitively, the proposed model is sufficiently abstract to specify any exam, from traditional to Internet-based exams. Traditional exams usually provide evidence data via log books and registers, while Internet-based exams implement the electronic versions, such as web bulletin boards.

Individual verifiability definitions consider a candidate who can check if she got a valid set of questions, if her test was properly processed through the phases of the exam, and if her mark was correctly computed. Universal verifiability definitions consider an external auditor who can check the correct execution of the exam with no private knowledge about the run of the exam. The auditor can verify if only registered candidates took the exam, if all tests were properly processed and marked, and if the marks were assigned correctly.

Generally speaking, the proposed formal frameworks bring exams to the attention of the security community. Computer-based exams are becoming widespread, and it can be difficult to discover exam protocol vulnerabilities as they may be exposed to unprecedented cheating attacks. The popularity of Internet-based exams are the next big challenge as concerns testing procedures, and verifiability assurance is required for their widespread acceptance. This chapter poses the first research step in the formal understanding of exam protocols. The analysis of the exams discussed in the following chapters aims at validating the proposed frameworks.

Chapter 4

The Huszti-Pethő Protocol

Although several exam systems are available, the Huszti-Pethő [HP10] exam was the first protocol proposed in the literature that focused on authentication and privacy requirements, even in the presence of corrupted candidates and exam authorities. Since no formal proof that guarantees the security of the protocol has been advanced so far, we take it as an opportunity to validate our model for secure exams.

Huszti and Pethő provided an informal analysis of their protocol with respect to six security requirements. Some requirements contain in turn other sub-requirements. For example, the requirement of *Secrecy* implicitly specifies two sub-requirements as it states that *"exam questions are kept secret"* and *"only the corresponding student should know his mark"*. Table 4.1 clarifies the sub-requirements and shows how to map them into the security requirements proposed in Chapter 3. The table indicates that combinations of our security requirements capture each of the informal requirements defined by Huszti and Pethő. For example, the informal definition of Robustness proposed by Huszti and Pethő, which says that questions can not be altered after submission, is captured by the combination of Answer Authenticity, Test Authenticity, and Mark Authenticity. We anticipate that the results of our analysis of the protocol demonstrates that it guarantees only one of our security requirements and none of the six requirements envisaged by Huszti and Pethő.

The Huszti-Pethő exam protocol uses four cryptographic building blocks: ElGamal encryption [EG85], zero-knowledge proof [GMR85], reusable anonymous return channel [GJ03], and a timed-release service based on Shamir's secret sharing [Sha79].

ElGamal Encryption

This cryptographic primitive for public-key cryptography consists of three algorithms of *key generation*, *encryption*, and *decryption*. The key generation algorithm outputs the public key $PK = (G, q, g, h)$ and the secret key $SK = s$; G is a cyclic group of order q with generator g; s is a random value in $\mathbb{Z}_q^*$; and $h = g^s$. The encryption algorithm takes in a message m and a random value $k \in \mathbb{Z}_q^*$, and outputs the ciphertext $(g^k, m \cdot h^k)$, which is denoted with $\{m\}_{PK}$. The decryption algorithm takes as input the ciphertext $\{m\}_{PK}$ and the secret key SK, and outputs the message m. In fact, $\frac{h^k}{g^{ks}} = \frac{g^{sk}}{g^{ks}} = m$. The ElGamal en-

© Springer International Publishing AG 2018
R. Giustolisi, *Modelling and Verification of Secure Exams*, Information Security and Cryptography, https://doi.org/10.1007/978-3-319-67107-9_4

Requirement	Huszti and Pethő Description	This book
Authenticity	*Only eligible students tests should be considered*	Candidate Authorisation Answer Authenticity
	It should be verified whether the exam grade is proposed by a teacher	Mark Authenticity
Anonymity	*Teachers do not know which paper belongs to which student when correcting*	Anonymous Marking
	Students do not know who corrects their papers	Anonymous Examiner
Secrecy	*Exam questions are kept secret*	Question Indistinguishability
	Only the corresponding student should know his mark	Mark Anonymity
Robustness	*Exam questions can not be altered after submission*	Answer Authenticity Test Authenticity Mark Authenticity
Correctness	*Students are not allowed to take the same exam more than once*	Answer Authenticity
Receipt	*Students are able to confirm a successful submission*	Answer Authenticity Test Authenticity Mark Authenticity

Table 4.1: Comparison of Huszti and Pethő's requirements with ones proposed in this book

cryption primitive is semantically secure assuming the decisional Diffie-Hellman problem is intractable.

Zero-knowledge Proof

This cryptographic scheme allows a *prover* to convince a *verifier* that a given statement is true without revealing any extra information except the correctness of the statement. A zero-knowledge scheme must guarantee completeness, soundness, and zero knowledge. Completeness means that if the statement is true, then the verifier always accepts the statement. Soundness means that if the statement is false, then the verifier always rejects the statement. Zero knowledge means that the verifier cannot get any information apart from the fact that the statement is indeed true.

Zero-knowledge schemes can be categorised into *interactive* and *non-interactive*. Interactive zero-knowledge proofs require prover and verifier to exchange at least two messages. The input of the prover is usually a challenge message sent by the verifier. In so doing, the proof is only valid for that challenge, and cannot be replayed by the prover to someone else.

Non-interactive zero-knowledge proof schemes contain only the message sent by a prover to the verifier. They are simpler and more efficient than interactive schemes, hence more suitable for the inclusion in the design of cryptographic protocols. In the remainder, we only consider non-interactive schemes as zero-knowledge proof.

Timed-Release Service

This service is based on threshold Shamir's secret sharing, a cryptographic primitive that ensures fixed-term secrecy. A secret is shared among n servers and cannot be reconstructed unless some servers collaborate to reveal the secret. Timed-release service assumes the existence of a trusted third party, which in the Huszti-Pethő protocol is known as *registry*. The registry knows the secret, bootstraps the knowledge of servers by sending them shares of the secret, and serves as authority to provide absolute time reference to the servers. The Huszti-Pethő protocol uses the timed-release service to deanonymise a candidate's pseudonym for notification. We do not detail this service further because in our security analysis of Huszti-Pethő we assume the servers to be trusted.

Outline of the chapter. Section 4.1 details the fundamentals of reusable anonymous return channel, the cryptographic scheme that the Huszti-Pethő protocol uses to guarantee anonymity. Section 4.2 describes the Huszti-Pethő protocol according to the four phases of an exam. Section 4.3 advances the security analysis in ProVerif of reusable anonymous return channel. Section 4.4 details the security analysis of the Huszti-Pethő protocol. Section 4.5 proposes amendments to the Huszti-Pethő protocol to improve its security. Section 4.6 concludes the chapter.

4.1 Reusable Anonymous Return Channel

We discuss in detail reusable anonymous return channel because this cryptographic scheme is less popular than ElGamal encryption and Zero-knowledge proof, and is at the core of the Huszti-Pethő protocol, in which *any* communication happens through this channel.

A reusable anonymous return channel implements anonymous two-way conversations between a *sender* and a *receiver* using a *mixer*. The mixer is implemented by a re-encryption mix network that consists of a chain of mix servers. The servers take in messages from multiple senders, randomly shuffle them, and send them to the receivers. Reusable anonymous return channel has two main goals:

- Ensure the anonymity of the sender

- Allow the receiver to reply to the sender while guaranteeing the anonymity of the sender

Note that a reusable anonymous return channel scheme aims to ensure anonymity, but not the secrecy of the messages [GJ03]. As we shall see, the Huszti-Pethő protocol resorts on this primitive for both message secrecy and sender anonymity.

Reusable anonymous return channel consists of five algorithms, namely *setup, submission of messages, delivery of messages, submission of replies*, and *delivery of replies*. The scheme assumes a primitive for digital signature, but the authors did not specify which one. However, digital signature primitives usually employ public-key cryptography and consist of three algorithms of *key generation, signing*, and *verification*. Key generation outputs the secret signing key SSK and verification public key SPK. The signing algorithm takes in a message m and the signing key SSK, and outputs the signature $Sign_{SSK}(m)$. The verification algorithm takes as input the signature $Sign_{SSK}(m)$ and the verification public key SPK, and returns **true** if the signature is correct, namely the message m was actually signed with the signing key SSK.

Setup. The setup algorithm consists of mix servers jointly generating an El-Gamal key pair (SK_M, PK_M), and signature keys (SSK_M, SPK_M). Sender and receiver also generate respectively the ElGamal pairs (PK_A, SK_A) and (PK_B, SK_B). The identities of the sender and the receiver are denoted respectively with the tags ID_A and ID_B. For example, email addresses can serve as an identity tag.

Submission of messages. The algorithm of the submission of messages is run by the sender A. It allows A to send an anonymous message m to the receiver with tag ID_B. The sender generates the triplet

$$(\{ID_A, PK_A\}_{PK_M}, \{m\}_{PK_M}, \{ID_B, PK_B\}_{PK_M})$$

and two *proofs of knowledge* of $\{ID_A, PK_A\}$ and of $\{ID_B, PK_B\}$. Proofs of knowledge are similar to zero-knowledge schemes but guarantee only completeness and soundness. In this case, they aim to avoid the attacker to decrypt the triplets by using the mixer as an oracle. The sender outputs the triplet and the proofs.

Delivery of messages. The mixer runs the algorithm of delivery of messages. It takes as input a batch of triplets and proofs sent from different senders. The mixer checks the proofs and then randomly shuffles the batch of triplets. Each triplet is extended with a checksum to ensure they are not separated during the shuffle. The message m is then re-encrypted with PK_B, resulting in the ciphertext $\{m\}_{PK_B}$. The mixer signs the first element of the triplet in input $\{ID_A, PK_A\}_{PK_M}$, and outputs the pair

$$(Sign_{SSK_M}(\{ID_A, PK_A\}_{PK_M}), \{m\}_{PK_B}).$$

Submission of replies. The receiver can reply an anonymous message with a new message m' using the algorithm for submission of replies. The receiver takes in the pair $(Sign_{SSK_M}(\{ID_A, PK_A\}_{PK_M}), \{m\}_{PK_B})$, encrypts the message m' with the public key of the mixnet PK_M resulting in m'_{PK_M}, and outputs the triplet

$$(\{ID_B, PK_B\}_{PK_M}, \{m'\}_{PK_M}, Sign_{SSK_M}(\{ID_A, PK_A\}_{PK_M}))$$

and the proof of knowledge of $\{ID_B, PK_B\}$.

Delivery of replies. The algorithm of delivery of reply is similar to one of delivery of messages. The only difference is that the input consists of the triplet $(\{ID_B, PK_B\}_{PK_M}, m'_{PK_M}, Sign_{SSK_M}(\{ID_A, PK_A\}_{PK_M}))$ and proof of knowledge of $\{ID_B, PK_B\}$, thus the mixer verifies only one proof of knowledge.

A succinct description of reusable anonymous return channel in the Alice-Bob notation is given in Figure 4.1.

1. $A{\rightarrow}M$: $\{ID_A, PK_A\}_{PK_M}, \{m\}_{PK_M}, \{ID_B, PK_B\}_{PK_M}$

2. $M{\rightarrow}B$: $Sign_{SSK_M}(\{ID_A, PK_A\}_{PK_M}), \{m\}_{PK_B}$

3. $B{\rightarrow}M$: $\{ID_B, PK_B\}_{PK_M}, \{m'\}_{PK_M}, Sign_{SSK_M}(\{ID_A, PK_A\}_{PK_M})$

Figure 4.1: Reusable anonymous return channel in the Alice-Bob notation

4.2   Protocol Description

The Huszti-Pethő protocol specifies six roles: exam authority (EA), registry, timed-release service (NET), question committee (COM), candidate (C), examiner (E). The exam authority manages the entire exam process. Specifically, it generates the pseudonyms to anonymise candidates' tests and examiner's identities, collects the tests, distributes the tests to examiners, and notifies the marks to the candidates. The registry generates the necessary cryptographic keys for the other roles and bootstraps the timed-release service. The NET consists of the servers that implement the timed-release service, and contributes to generate and revoke the candidate pseudonyms using threshold Shamir's secret sharing. The question committee generates the questions for the exam, the candidate takes the exam, and the examiner marks the tests.

The protocol assumes that no candidate reveals their private keys to other candidates, and that invigilators supervise candidates during the testing phase. All communications take place via reusable anonymous return channels.

The protocol originally sees three stages: *registration*, *exam*, and *grading*. It can be observed that the exam stage begins with the exam authority checking the candidate's eligibility, and concludes with the examiner sending the mark to the exam authority. Thus, to match this structure with our phases, we map the registration stage to preparation, the grading stage to notification, and we divide the exam stage in testing and marking. We provide a high-level description of the protocol, which is supported by a more detailed specification in the Alice-Bob notation in Figure 4.2.

Preparation

This phase concerns the registration of both candidate and examiner, and the generation of the pseudonyms. The exam authority publishes the public parameters to identify a new exam (step 1). The question committee then signs and sends the questions, which are encrypted with the public key of the mixer implementing the reusable anonymous return channel (step 2). The mixer will publish the questions only at time of testing ($time_1$).

The registration of the examiner consists of creating a pseudonym, which is jointly generated by the exam authority and the examiner. The examiner verifies the correctness of the pseudonym by using a zero-knowledge proof (ZKP_{eq}) on the equality of the discrete logarithms with the exam authority (step 6). To enrol for an exam, the examiner sends pseudonym and subject to the exam authority (step 9), and proves the knowledge of his secret key ($ZKP_{sec}(SK_E)$). Note that the exam authority knows that the examiner is eligible for the exam, but cannot

Preparation

1. EA publishes g and $h = g^s$

2. $COM \to EA : \{Sign_{SSK_{COM}}(question, time_1)\}_{PK_M}$

3. EA checks E eligibility, and calculates $\tilde{q} = PK_E^s$ //Examiner Registration

4. $EA \to E : \tilde{q}, g_E$

5. E calculates $q' = (\tilde{q})^\alpha$, $t = (g_E)^\alpha$, and $q = t^{SK_E}$

6. $EA \leftrightarrow E : ZKP_{eq}((q, q'), (g, h))$ //E pseudonym is (t, q, q')

7. $E \to EA : t, q, q', subject$

8. EA checks $q^s = q'$

9. $E \leftrightarrow EA : ZKP_{sec}(SK_E)$

10. EA stores ZKP data plus $\{ID_E, PK_E\}_{PK_M}$ and $subject$

11. EA checks C eligibility, and calculates $\tilde{p} = (PK_C)^s$ //Candidate Registration

12. $EA \to NET : \tilde{p}, g_C$

13. NET calculates $p' = (\tilde{p})^\Gamma$, and $r = (g_C)^\Gamma$, and stores $time$ of notification, $\tilde{p}$, and g_C.

14. $NET \to C : r, p'$

15. C calculates $p = r^{SK_C}$

16. $EA \leftrightarrow C : ZKP_{eq}((p, p'), (g, h))$ //C pseudonym is (r, p, p')

Testing

17. $C \to EA : r, p, p', subject$

18. EA checks $p^s = p'$

19. $C \leftrightarrow EA : ZKP_{sec}(SK_C)$

20. $EA \to C : Sign_{SSK_{COM}}(question), time_1$

21. $C \to EA : r, p, \{answer\}_{PK_M}, time_2$

22. $EA \to C : Hash(r, p, p', subject, trans_C, question, time_1, time_2, \{answer\}_{PK_M})$

Marking

23. $EA \to E : \{answer\}_{PK_M}$

24. $E \to EA : mark, Hash(mark, answer), [Hash(mark, answer)]^{SK_E}, verzkp$
    where $verzkp = ZKP_{eq}(Hash(mark, answer), [Hash(mark, answer)]^{SK_E}), t, q$

Notification

26. $EA \to NET : p'$ // Note that $r = (g_C)^\Gamma$, $p = (PK_C)^\Gamma$, $p' = (g_C)^{\Gamma s}$

27. NET calculates $p' = (\tilde{p})^\Gamma$

28. $NET \to EA : \{p', \tilde{p}\}_{PK_{EA}}$

29. EA stores $mark, Hash(mark, answer), [Hash(mark, answer)]^{SK_E}, verzkp$

Figure 4.2: The Huszti-Pethő e-exam protocol in the Alice-Bob notation

learn the examiner identity since the communication takes place via reusable anonymous return channel. Thus, at the end of examiner registration, the exam authority stores the encrypted identity of the examiner ($\{ID_E, PK_E\}_{PK_M}$) (step 10), which the exam authority will use to send the answer to the anonymous examiner at marking.

The registration of a candidate slightly differs from the registration of an examiner since the anonymity of the candidate eventually will be broken at notification, while the anonymity of examiner may last forever. The pseudonym of the candidate is jointly calculated by the exam authority, the candidate, and also the NET. The NET stores the secret values used for the generation of the candidate pseudonym (step 13), and will use the secret values at notification to allow the exam authority to associate the candidate with the mark. Similarly to the registration of examiner, the candidate can verify the correctness of the pseudonym using a zero-knowledge proof (ZKP_{eq}) of the equality of the discrete logarithms with the exam authority being the prover (step 16).

Testing

The candidate sends the pseudonym to the exam authority (step 17) and proves the knowledge of the private key ($ZKP_{sec}(SK_C)$) (step 19). We stress that the protocol assumes the candidate does not share with other principals the private key. The exam authority checks whether the pseudonym is allowed for the exam (step 18), and then sends the questions signed by the question committee (step 20). The candidate then sends the answer (step 21) encrypted with the public key of the mixer ($\{answer\}_{PK_M}$). At marking, the mixer will re-encrypt the answer with the public key of the examiner. Thus, the exam authority cannot learn the answer submitted by the candidate. Testing concludes with the exam authority sending to the candidate a receipt (step 22), which consists of the hash of all parameters seen by the exam authority during testing, the transcription of the zero-knowledge proof ($trans_C$), and the time when the answer was submitted ($time_2$).

Marking

We recall that at preparation the exam authority stored the encrypted identities of the examiners, thus it can choose an examiner who is eligible for the exam to forwards the candidate's answer. The examiner assigns the answer with a mark (step 23), and sends it to the exam authority with a zero-knowledge proof ($verzkp$), which proves the examiner actually marked the answer (step 24).

Notification

When all the answers are marked, the NET de-anonymises the pseudonyms associated to the answers, so the exam authority can link back the pseudonym with the corresponding candidate (steps 27-28). Finally, the exam authority stores the marks and the zero-knowledge proof provided at marking by the examiner (step 29).

4.3 Security of Reusable Anonymous Return Channel

Prior to verifying the Huszti-Pethő protocol, we provide a formal analysis of reusable anonymous return channel. In particular, we verify whether the scheme ensures message secrecy and anonymity of sender and receiver as it is assumed in the Huszti-Pethő protocol.

Model Choices

The equational theory in Table 4.2 models the cryptographic primitives for reusable anonymous return channel. It includes models for ElGamal public-key encryption, digital signatures, and zero-knowledge proof. ElGamal encryption consists of two functions *encryption* and *decryption*. A message encrypted with a public key can only be decrypted using the corresponding secret key. The functionality of digital signatures is modelled with two equations: the function *getmess* checks integrity as it returns a message embedded into a signature; the function *checksign* checks also for authenticity as it returns the message only if the function is provided with the correct verification key. The theory for zero-knowledge proof that we use is inspired by Backes *et al.* [BMU08], who model zero-knowledge proof as two functions. The function *zkp_proof* models the proof that the prover builds to demonstrate the knowledge of the secret, which in the case of reusable anonymous return channel is the message encrypted with the public key of the mixer. The function *zkpsec* models the verification of the proof by the verifier, which in the case of reusable anonymous return channel is the mixer. The function *zkp_proof(public, secret)* takes as arguments public and secret parameters. In this case, the public parameter is the encryption of the message, and the private parameter is the message. Note that the correct function can be constructed only by the prover who knows the private parameter. The verification function *zkpsec(zkp_proof(public, secret), verinfo)* takes as arguments the proof function and the verification parameter *verinfo*. The verifier only accepts the proof if the relation between *verinfo* and *secret* is satisfied.

The ProVerif description of sender, receivers, and mixer processes is outlined in Figure 4.3. We specify one sender and two receivers, and model a simpler version of reusable anonymous return channel without considering the submission of reply, namely we omit step 3 of Figure 4.1. As we shall see later, this simpler version is sufficient to show successful attacks on message secrecy and sender anonymity.

An instance of reusable anonymous return channel is in Figure 4.4. We recall that submission of a message consists of the triplet $(\{ID_A, PK_A\}_{PK_M}, \{m\}_{PK_M}, \{ID_B, PK_B\}_{PK_M})$. We use the choice command in ProVerif to check both message secrecy and sender anonymity. This command allows us to verify if the processes obtained by instantiating a variable with two different values are bisimilar.

We analyse secrecy of the message by checking whether the attacker can distinguish the two scenarios in which the sender outputs two different messages. Thus, choice is applied in the second element of the triplet, and the process of the sender becomes as in Figure 4.5.

We analyse anonymity of the sender by checking whether the attacker can say if the message is sent either to Receiver 1 or Receiver 2. In this case, choice

```
(*----Sender----*)
let A (SKa: skey, PKb: pkey, PKmix: pkey, SPKmix: spkey) =
 out(c, (encrypt(pkey_to_bitstring(pk(SKa)), PKmix),
         encrypt(secret_message, PKmix),
         encrypt(pkey_to_bitstring(PKb), PKmix))).

(*----Receiver 1----*)
let B (SKb: skey, PKmix: pkey, SPKmix: spkey) =
 in (c, (c1: bitstring , s1: bitstring, cm1: bitstring)).

(*----Receiver 2----------------------*)
let C (SKc: skey, PKmix: pkey, SPKmix: spkey) =
 in (c, (c1: bitstring , s1: bitstring, cm1: bitstring)).

(*----Mixer----*)
let MIX (SKmix: skey, SSKmix: sskey ) =
 !MIX1(SKmix, SSKmix) | !MIX2(SKmix, SSKmix).

(*----Mixer 1----*)
let MIX1 (SKmix: skey, SSKmix: sskey ) =
 in (c, (c1: bitstring, c2: bitstring, c3: bitstring,
         p1:zkp, p2:zkp));
 let (xmsg: bitstring) = decrypt(c2, SKmix) in
 let (xdst: pkey) = bitstring_to_pkey(decrypt(c3, SKmix)) in
 if(checkproof(p1,c1) && checkproof(p2,c3)) then
  (out(c, (c1, sign(c1, SSKmix), encrypt( xmsg, xdst)))).

(*----Mixer 2----*)
let MIX2 (SKmix: skey, SSKmix: sskey ) =
 in (c, (c1': bitstring, c2': bitstring, c3': bitstring,
         p1':zkp, p2':bitstring));
 let (xmsg': bitstring) = decrypt(c2', SKmix) in
 let (xdst': pkey) = bitstring_to_pkey(decrypt(c3', SKmix)) in
 if(checkproof(p1',c1') && checksign(p2',spk(SSKmix)) = c3') then
  (out(c, (c1', sign(c1', SSKmix), encrypt( xmsg', xdst')))).
```

Figure 4.3: The processes of sender, receivers, and mixer

is applied in the first element of the triplet. Figure 4.6 shows the process of the sender to check anonymity.

Results

The results of the automatic analysis in ProVerif indicate that reusable anonymous return channel fails to guarantee both secrecy of messages and anonymity of sender and receiver identities. According to the attack traces generated by ProVerif, both message secrecy and sender anonymity can be exploited using the same attack strategy. The attacker can use the mixer as decryption oracle,

```
process
 new skA: skey; let pkA = pk(skA) in out (c, pkA);
 new skB: skey; let pkB = pk(skB) in out (c, pkB);
 new skC: skey; let pkC = pk(skC) in out (c, pkC);
 new skMIX: skey; let pkMIX = pk(skMIX) in out (c, pkMIX);
 new sskMIX: sskey; let spkMIX = spk(sskMIX) in out (c, spkMIX);
 (
        (A(skA, pkB, pkMIX, spkMIX)) |
        (B(skB, pkMIX, spkMIX)) |
        (C(skC, pkMIX, spkMIX)) |
        (MIX(skMIX, sskMIX))
 )
```

Figure 4.4: The instance of sender, receiver, and mixer processes

```
(*----Sender----*)
let A (SKa: skey, PKb: pkey, PKmix: pkey, SPKmix: spkey) =
 out(c, (encrypt(pkey_to_bitstring(pk(SKa)), PKmix),
        encrypt(choice[secret_message1, secret_message2], PKmix),
        encrypt(pkey_to_bitstring(PKb), PKmix))).
```

Figure 4.5: The instance of sender to analyse message secrecy

```
(*----Sender----*)
let A (SKa: skey, SKb:skey, PKb: pkey, PKc: pkey,
       PKmix: pkey, SPKmix: spkey) =
 out(c, (encrypt(pkey_to_bitstring(pk(choice[SKa, SKb])), PKmix),
        encrypt(secret_message, PKmix),
        encrypt(pkey_to_bitstring(PKb), PKmix))).
```

Figure 4.6: The instance of sender to analyse anonymity

1. $A{\rightarrow}M$: $\{ID_A, PK_A\}_{PK_M}, \{m\}_{PK_M}, \{ID_B, PK_B\}_{PK_M}$

2. $I{\rightarrow}M$: $\{ID_A, PK_A\}_{PK_M}, \{ID_A, PK_A\}_{PK_M}, \{ID_I, PK_I\}_{PK_M}$

3. $M{\rightarrow}I$: $Sign_{SSK_M}(\{ID_A, PK_A\}_{PK_M}), \{ID_A, PK_A\}_{PK_I}$

Figure 4.7: Attack trace on sender anonymity

Primitive	Equation
ElGamal encryption	$decrypt(encrypt(m, pk(sk), r), sk) = m$
Digital signature	$getmess(sign(m, ssk)) = m$
	$checksign(sign(m, ssk), spk(ssk)) = m$
Zero-knowledge proof	$zkpsec(zkp\_proof(encrypt(m, pk(sk), r), (r, m)),$
	$encrypt(m, pk(sk), r)) = true$

Table 4.2: Equational theory to model reusable anonymous return channel

letting the mixer reveal any of the plaintexts contained in the triplet. The zero-knowledge proofs required to avoid this very attack reveal to be insufficient. In fact, the attack traces provided by ProVerif show the attacker can input the mixer with valid zero-knowledge proofs.

In the following we detail the attack traces. The attacker chooses one of the three elements of the triplet. This choice depends on what the attacker wants to learn: if the target is the content of the message, the attacker chooses the second element; if the target is the identity of the sender, the attacker chooses the first element; if the target is the identity of the receiver, the attacker chooses the third element. Whatever the element of the triplet, the attacker submits this as a new message.

Figure 4.7 shows how the attacker can defeat sender anonymity. The attacker targets $\{ID_A, PK_A\}_{PK_M}$, which becomes the second element of the new triplet submitted by the attacker. Note that the attacker can leave the first element of the triplet and the zero-knowledge proof unchanged. The attacker replaces the third element of the triplet with a public key PK_I for which the attacker knows the corresponding secret key SK_I. Thus, the attacker can also provide the necessary proof of knowledge of the plaintext contained in the third element. The mixer then shuffles the input messages, and encrypts the message with the attacker public key. Since the attacker knows the secret key SK_I, he can decrypt the message, which in this case is ID_A, PK_A, namely the identity of the sender.

Since the attacker can substitute any of the elements of the triplet as a new message, reusable anonymous return channel can neither ensure secrecy of the messages nor anonymity of sender and receiver. It can be observed that the checksum meant to guarantee the integrity of the triplet is added after the submission of the triplet, and is only used inside the mixer. Hence, the checksum does not prevent the attacker from submitting a modified triplet. Unfortunately even adding the checksum before the submission of the triplet does not prevent the attack as the knowledge of the ciphertexts is sufficient to compute the checksum.

Remark. Reusable anonymous return channel was originally designed to withstand a passive attacker that however can statically corrupt parties [GJ03]. Our analysis in ProVerif considers an active attacker. We observe that a passive attacker is not realistic in exam, where corrupted principals could actively try to cheat. However, an attacker who statically corrupts principals can still defeat reusable anonymous return channel. A corrupted principal can be instructed to

Primitive	Equation
ElGamal encryption	$decrypt(encrypt(m, pk(sk), r), sk) = m$
Digital signature	$getmess(sign(m, ssk)) = m$ $checksign(sign(m, ssk), spk(ssk)) = m$
Zero-knowledge proof	$zkpsec(zkp\_proof(exp(exp(g, e1), e2), e2),$ $exp(exp(g, e1), e2)) = true$
Diffie-Hellman exp.	$exp(exp(exp(g, x), y), z) = exp(exp(exp(g, y), z), x)$
ZKP of discrete log.	$checkproof(xproof(p, p', t, exp(t, e), e),$ $p, p', t, exp(t, e)) = true$

Table 4.3: Equational theory to model the Huszti-Pethő protocol

send and receive messages via the reusable anonymous return channel on behalf of the attacker. The attacker still need to intercept those messages before they enter the mixer, but this is possible with insecure networks such as the Internet.

4.4 Security of the Huszti-Pethő Protocol

We now introduce the formal model of the Huszti-Pethő protocol and then the results of the analysis of authentication and privacy.

Model Choices

The first choice about how to model the protocol concerns the communication channels. The Huszti-Pethő protocol assumes that all messages are exchanged using a reusable anonymous return channel. In the previous section, we demonstrated that reusable anonymous return channel fails to guarantee both message secrecy and sender anonymity. We choose to model the Huszti-Pethő protocol with the *ideal* implementation of reusable anonymous return channel, which guarantees anonymity of senders and receivers. This can be implemented with ProVerif's anonymous channels.

The equational theory depicted in Table 4.3 models the cryptographic primitives used within the Huszti-Pethő protocol. It includes the same models of ElGamal encryption, digital signatures, and zero-knowledge proofs defined for reusable anonymous return channels. In addition, we provide an equation to model the Diffie-Hellmann exponentiation. This model is limited as it just takes into account the equation needed for the protocol to work, and does not capture the full set of algebraic properties of Diffie-Hellmann exponentiation that an attacker may exploit to break the protocol. However, this has a limited influence on our analysis because, as we shall see later, the protocol ensures only one out of ten security requirements, namely nine requirements cannot be met as the attacker can break the protocol without resorting to the algebraic properties of Diffie-Hellmann exponentiation.

The equations for zero-knowledge proofs are customised according to the exponentiation operator. In particular, we support the model of zero-knowledge proof of the equality of discrete logarithms *check_proof* with tables in ProVerif. We resort on tables because ProVerif cannot deal with the associativity of mul-

Requirement	Result	Time
Candidate Authorisation	✓	26 s
Answer Authenticity	×	3 s
Test Origin Authentication	×	3 s
Test Authenticity	×	33 s
Mark Authenticity	×	52 s
Question Indistinguishability	×	< 1 s
Anonymous Marking	×	1h 58 m 33 s
Anonymous Examiner	×	6h 37 m 33 s
Mark Privacy	×	23 m 59 s
Mark Anonymity	×	49 m 5 s

Table 4.4: Summary of the analysis of the Huszti-Pethő protocol

tiple exponents. This approach is sound because it limits the attacker capability to generate fake zero-knowledge proofs, since the attacker cannot write and read ProVerif tables.

We assume that the same generator g is used to generate the pseudonyms of candidates and examiners. Also this choice is sound because we distinguish the roles, and each principal is identified by its public key. We replace the candidate identity with the corresponding pseudonym inside the events to check authentication requirements. Note that the replacement is also sound because the equational theory preserves the bijective mapping between the keys that identify the candidates and the pseudonyms.

The process of the exam authority is modelled as in Figures 4.8 and 4.9. It is conveniently split into four subprocesses. Three subprocesses concern preparation and consist of the initialisation of the exam authority, the registration of the candidate, the registration of the examiner. The last subprocess concerns the remaining phases, namely testing, marking, and notification.

The ProVerif model of the candidate is depicted in Figure 4.10, the examiner process is in Figure 4.11, the NET process is in Figure 4.12, and the exam process is modelled as in Figure 4.13. All the processes are augmented with the events that allow verifying the authentication requirements. To verify Question Indistinguishability we use the **noninterf** command of ProVerif, which checks that any two instances of the exam protocol that only differ in the value of the variable of questions are bisimilar. To verify Mark Privacy, Anonymous Examiner and Anonymous Marking we use the ProVerif command **choice[]**.

The full ProVerif code used to analyse the requirements of the Huszti-Pethő protocol is available upon request from the author.

Results

The analysis in ProVerif shows that the Huszti-Pethő protocol only ensures Candidate Authorisation as reported in Table 4.4. Regarding Answer Authenticity, ProVerif shows an attack trace that allows the exam authority to accept a test that has not been submitted by a registered candidate. In fact, the attacker can generate a fake pseudonym that allows him to take part in an exam for which the attacker did not register. This is possible because the exam authority

```
let EAi (SSKea: sskey,  SPKcom: spkey) =
(*Preparation*)
new s: exponent;
let h=exp(g, s) in
let sh=sign(h,SSKea) in
out(c, (h,sh));
in(c, (quest: bitstring, squest: bitstring));
(!Ereg(h,s) | !Creg(h,s,quest,squest, SPKcom, SSKea)).

let Ereg (h: bitstring, s: exponent)=
(* Examiner Registration *)
get keys (=g_e, xpk_e) in
let q_tilde=exp(xpk_e, s) in
out(c, (q_tilde, xpk_e));
insert zkpeq(q_tilde, xpk_e);
(* EA inserts q_tilde into a table to support the zkp with E *)
in(c, (q: bitstring, q': bitstring));
out(c, xproof(q,q',g, h, s));
in (c, (t: bitstring, =q, =q'));
if exp(q,s)=q' then
  in(c, zkp_sec_proof: bitstring);
  if zkpsec2(zkp_sec_proof,t, q)=true then 0.

let Creg (h: bitstring, s: exponent, quest: bitstring,
          squest: bitstring,  SPKcom: spkey, sskea:sskey)=
(* Candidate Registration *)
get keys (=g_c, xpk_c) in
let p_tilde=exp(xpk_c, s) in
insert reg_cand(xpk_c, p_tilde, h);
out(c, (p_tilde, g_c));
(* EA inserts p_tilde into a table to support the zkp with C *)
insert zkpeq(p_tilde, xpk_c);
in(c, (p: bitstring, p': bitstring));
(* EA registered C with pseudonym 'p' to the exam 'h' *)
out(c, xproof(p,p',g, h, s));
Exam(h,s,quest,squest, SPKcom,sskea).
```

Figure 4.8: The process of the exam authority that concerns preparation

```
let Exam (h: bitstring, s: exponent, quest: bitstring,
            squest: bitstring, SPKcom: spkey, SSKea: sskey)=
(*Testing*)
 in (c, (r: bitstring,p: bitstring,p':bitstring));
 if exp(p,s)=p' then
  in (c, zkp_sec_proof: bitstring);
  if zkpsec2(zkp_sec_proof, r, p)=true then
   if quest=checksign(squest, SPKcom) then
    out(c, (quest, squest));
    in (c, (=r, =p, answer: bitstring));
    (* EA succesfully collects the pair ('quest','answer') *)
    (* from C with pseudonym 'p' for the exam 'h' *)
    event collected(p', h, quest, answer);
    out(c,  hash( (r, p, p', zkp_sec_proof, quest, answer)));

(*Marking*)
    (* EA chooses an E who registered for the exam 'h' *)
    get examinertable(t, q, =h, xzkp_sec_proof) in
    new eap: bitstring;
    (* EA assigns 'eap' to the pair ('quest','answer') *)
    (* submitted by C with pseudonym 'p' for the exam 'h',*)
    (* and distributes them to E with pseudonym 'q' *)
    event distributed(p',h, quest, answer, eap, q);
    out(c, (eap, answer));
    get zkpeq(hma,=spkeytobitstring(spk(SSKea))) in
    in (c, (mark: bitstring, =hma, hma_e_enc: bitstring,
    zkp_sec_hma: bitstring, =t, =q));
    if (checkproof(zkp_sec_hma, hma, hma_e_enc,t,q)=true) then
     out(c, p');
(*Notification*)
     in (c, (=p', p_tilde: bitstring));
     get reg_cand(xpk_c, =p_tilde, =h) in
     insert marks(xpk_c,mark, hma, hma_e_enc, zkp_sec_hma, t,q).
```

Figure 4.9: The process of the exam authority that concerns testing, marking, and notification

```
let C (SKc: skey, SPKea: spkey, SPKcom: spkey) =
(*Preparation*)
 in (c, (h: bitstring, sh: bitstring));
 if h=checksign(sh, SPKea) then
  (* The zkp of equivalence of discrete log is supported by *)
  (* the tables 'zkpeq' and 'zkpeqnet'. *)
  (* In doing so, C can verify that 'ea_tilde' and 'p_tilde' *)
  (* have been correctly generated resp. by EA and NET *)
  get zkpeq(ea_tilde, =exp(g,skey_to_exponent(SKc))) in
  get zkpeqnet(=ea_tilde,r,p') in
  let p=exp(r,skey_to_exponent(SKc)) in
  out(c, (p, p'));
  in (c, zproof: bitstring);
  if (checkproof(zproof, p, p',g,h)=true) then
   let zkp_sec_c = zkp_proof2(r,p,skey_to_exponent(SKc)) in
   out(c, (r,p,p'));
   out(c, zkp_sec_c);

(*Testing*)
   in (c, (quest: bitstring, squest: bitstring));
   if quest=checksign(squest, SPKcom) then
    new answ: bitstring;
    (* C submits 'answ' and 'quest' for the exam 'h' *)
    event submitted(p', h, quest, answ);
    out(c, (r, p, answ));
    in (c, receipt: bitstring);
    if (hash( (r,p,p', zkp_sec_c, quest, answ))=receipt) then

(*Notification*)
     get marks(=exp(g,skey_to_exponent(SKc)),mark, hma, hma_e_enc,
     zkp_sec_hma, t,q) in
     get zkpeq(=hma,=spkeytobitstring(SPKea)) in
     if (hash((mark, answ)) = hma && checkproof(zkp_sec_hma, hma,
      hma_e_enc,t,q)=true ) then
       (* C is notified with 'mark' for the exam 'h' *)
       event notified(p',h,mark).
```

Figure 4.10: The process of the candidate

```
let E (SKe: skey,  SPKea: spkey, SPKcom: spkey) =
 (*Preparation*)
 in (c, (h: bitstring, sh: bitstring));
 if h=checksign(sh, SPKea) then
  new alpha: exponent;
  get zkpeq(q_tilde, =exp(g,skey_to_exponent(SKe))) in
  let q'=exp(q_tilde, alpha) in
  let t=exp(g, alpha) in
  let q=exp(t, skey_to_exponent(SKe)) in
  out (c, (q, q'));
  in (c, zproof: bitstring);
  if (checkproof(zproof, q, q',g,h)=true) then
   let zkp_sec_e = zkp_proof2(t,q,skey_to_exponent(SKe)) in
   out(c, (t,q,q'));
   out(c, zkp_sec_e);
   insert examinertable (t, q, h, zkp_sec_e);

  (*Marking*)
  in (c, (quest: bitstring, squest: bitstring));
  if quest=checksign(squest, SPKcom) then
   in (c, (eap: bitstring, answer: bitstring));
   new mark: bitstring;
   event marked(quest, answer, mark, eap, q, h);
   let hma=hash( (mark, answer) ) in
   let hma_e= exp(hma, skey_to_exponent(SKe)) in
   insert zkpeq(hma, spkeytobitstring(SPKea));
   let zkp_sec_hma=xproof(hma,hma_e,t,q,skey_to_exponent(SKe)) in
   out(c, (mark, hma, hma_e, zkp_sec_hma, t, q)).
```

Figure 4.11: The process of the examiner

```
let NET () =
(*Preparation*)
 in (c, (p_tilde: bitstring, =g_c));
 new ro: exponent;
 let p'=exp(p_tilde, ro) in
 let r=exp(g, ro) in
 (* The NET registered the candidate with pseudonym p' *)
 event registered(p');
 out(c,(p', r));
 (* The NET inserts 'p_tilde' into a table to support *)
 (* the zkp between EA (the prover) and C (the verifier) *)
 insert zkpeqnet(p_tilde,r,p');

(*Notification*)
 in (c, =p');
 out(c, (p', p_tilde)).
```

Figure 4.12: The process of the NET

```
process
 !(
 new sskEA: sskey; let spkEA = spk(sskEA) in out (c, spkEA);
 new sskCom: sskey; let spkCom = spk(sskCom) in out (c, spkCom);
 new question: bitstring;
 let squestion=sign(question, sskCom) in
 out(c, (question, squestion));

 !(new skC: skey; let pkC = exp(g,skey_to_exponent(skC)) in
   out (c, pkC); insert keys(g_c, pkC); C(skC, spkEA, spkCom)
  )|
 !(EAi(sskEA , spkCom))|
 !(new skE: skey; let pkE = exp(g,skey_to_exponent(skE))
   in out (c, pkE); insert keys(g_e, pkE); E(skE,   spkEA, spkCom)
  )|
 !(NET())
 )
```

Figure 4.13: The exam process

does not check whether the pseudonym has been actually created using the partial information provided by the NET. The attacker generates a secret key SK_I, and calculates an associate pseudonym, which sends to the exam authority. The exam authority successfully verifies the received data since the attacker knows SK_I, hence the exam authority accepts the test. In other words, the exam authority may collect a test whose pseudonym is replaced with one chosen by the attacker. The same attack trace violates Test Origin Authentication because the attacker can generate a valid pseudonym for a candidate who did not register for the exam.

ProVerif finds a counterexample that invalidates Test Authenticity. The requirement cannot be achieved because there is no mechanism that allows the examiner to check whether the answers have been forwarded by the exam authority. Although the answer is encrypted with the public key of the mixer, this does not guarantee that the exam authority actually sent the message, because anyone can submit any message to the mixer.

Regarding Mark Authenticity, ProVerif provides an attack trace in which the attacker can forward any answer to any examiner, even if the answer was not collected by the exam authority. Moreover, no mechanism ensures that the notified mark originates from the exam authority. In fact, the attacker can notify the candidate by himself with a mark of his choice.

The Huszti-Pethő exam protocol does not guarantee any privacy requirement. Intuitively, all privacy requirements can be violated because reusable anonymous return channel does not guarantee anonymity.

However, even assuming anonymous channels, ProVerif shows an attack trace for each requirement. Question Indistinguishability does not hold because messages sent via reusable anonymous return channel are not secret, as our analysis demonstrates. Since the questions are sent through the anonymous channel, the attacker can still obtain them.

Anonymous Marking is violated since the attacker can check whether a candidate accepts the zero-knowledge proof, hence associates the candidate identity with the pseudonym, and then identifies the candidate's test.

Anonymous Examiner can be also violated because the attacker can track which examiner accepts the zero-knowledge proof when receiving the partial pseudonym, hence associates the answer to the examiner.

Mark Privacy fails because the examiner sends the mark to the exam authority via reusable anonymous return channel, which does not ensure secrecy.

Finally, ProVerif shows that the Huszti-Pethő protocol does not also ensure Mark Anonymity. Since one can track which pseudonym is assigned to the candidate, and the mark is not secret, the attacker can link the candidate to the assigned mark.

4.5 Fixing Authentication

We observe that the Huszti-Pethő protocol fails to meet authentication mainly because two bad design choices:

- It makes an excessive use of RARC, which is used even when anonymity is not required;

- It lacks of explicitness in some message contents.

Requirement	Result	Time
Candidate Authorisation	✓	3 s
Answer Authenticity	×	2 s
Test Origin Authentication	✓	2 s
Test Authenticity	✓	3 s
Mark Authenticity	✓	4 s

Table 4.5: Summary of the analysis of authentication of the modified Huszti-Pethő protocol

Thus, we propose four modifications to the Huszti-Pethő protocol in order to achieve most of authentication requirement. In particular, we prove in ProVerif that the modified Huszti-Pethő protocol achieves Candidate Authorisation, Test Origin Authentication, Test Authenticity, and Mark Authenticity as in Table 4.5. We found no easy solution for Answer Authenticity because the protocol sees no signatures for candidates, and reusable anonymous return channel does not guarantee authentication.

Authenticate the channel/1. The first modification consists in the NET receiving the partial pseudonyms generated by the exam authority via a secure authenticated channel instead via reusable anonymous return channel. There is no need for the exam authority and the NET to communicate anonymously, hence via RARC as the original protocol prescribes. Conversely, they need a secure channel to stop an attacker to inject messages. In doing so, the attacker cannot use the NET to generate fake pseudonyms.

Authenticate the channel/2. For the same reasons outlined above, the second modification consists in the exam authority receiving the eligible pseudonyms from NET via a secure authenticated channel. Thus, the exam authority generates zero-knowledge proofs of the equality of discrete logarithm to eligible pseudonyms only. The exam authority can also store the eligible pseudonyms, which can be checked at testing before the exam authority accepts a test from a candidate.

Sign the tests. The third modification concerns marking, and consists in the exam authority signing the collected test prior to distribute it to the chosen examiner. In fact, while it is desirable that the examiner identity is not revealed, the exam authority identity can be revealed. Thus, the examiner marks the test only if after a successful validation of the exam authority signature on the test. In the original protocol, the examiner cannot verify whether a test was sent by the exam authority.

Report the test identifier. The last modification concerns the test identifier that is affixed by the exam authority to the test before distributing it to the examiner. This modification consists in a revised receipt of candidate's submission. The exam authority adds the test identifier to the receipt and signs it. The examiner also adds the test identifier into the receipt of marking, hence the candidates can verify whether they are notified with the correct marks.

In the original protocol, the attacker can notify the candidate with any other examiner's mark because the candidate is unaware of the test identifier.

Table 4.4 summarises the results of the formal analysis of the Huszti-Pethő protocol assuming all principal being honest.   The reported times refer to ProVerif analyses over an Intel Core i7 3.0 GHz machine with 8 GB RAM.

It can be seen that the modified Huszti-Pethő protocol guarantees four out five authentication requirements. Unfortunately, no easy solution can be envisaged for privacy. The design of the original protocol is heavily based on the assumption that reusable anonymous return channel guarantees secrecy, authentication, and anonymity. Since reusable anonymous return channel guarantees none of these properties, the Huszti-Pethő protocol would need a complete redesign to achieve privacy.

4.6   Conclusion

The Huszti-Pethő protocol was the first exam scheme proposed in the literature that was considered for a formal analysis of authentication and privacy requirements. The analysis of the protocol, although being quite complex, validates the framework proposed in the earlier chapters. It is found that the protocol guarantees only one of the eleven requirements. Authentication is compromised because of inaccuracies in the protocol design. Privacy requirements are mostly violated because of assumptions on the reusable anonymous return channel: it is demonstrated that an attacker can compromise message secrecy and anonymity on a reusable anonymous return channel.

A few modifications to the Huszti-Pethő protocol are introduced to meet most of the authentication requirements. The formal analysis in ProVerif confirms that the modified protocol ensures these requirements. We also demonstrate that the Huszti-Pethő protocol does not guarantee any privacy requirement even with an ideal implementation of the reusable anonymous return channel that guarantees sender anonymity. It means that the protocol requires some additional changes to meet all the requirements.

Chapter 5

The Remark! Internet-Based Exam

In this chapter, we introduce Remark!, a protocol designed for secure Internet-based exams. Remark! runs fully on computers to execute typical local tasks, such as the generation of questions and automatic marking, as well as remote tasks, such as remote registration and remote notification of candidates. Notably, it supports remote testing, in which distantly located candidates take the exam at their place, which is the distinctive functionality of Internet-based exams.

The goal of Remark! is to guarantee several authentication, privacy, and verifiability requirements without relying on a single trusted authority. The fundamental aim of its design is to distribute the trust among the parties and to get rid of TTP. This design approach is novel in the context of exam protocols because their design has normally been conceived with a TTP. However, the use of computers exposes exams to new threats and requires us to change the well-established procedures used in traditional exams. The conflicting interests that roles typically have in an exam complicate the design of secure exam protocols further. In fact, TTP may be corrupted, as recent scandals confirm [Cop13, Wat14, Lip14].

Remark! distributes the trust across the several servers that compose an *exponentiation mixnet*. As we shall see later, the mixnet generates the pseudonyms that allow the exam principals to encrypt and sign messages anonymously. Using ProVerif, we prove that Remark! ensures all the authentication and privacy requirements proposed in Chapter 3, with minimal reliance on trusted parties. Additionaly, we demonstrate that Remark! provides the verifiability-tests listed in the same chapter, and discuss the necessary assumptions to make Remark! fully verifiable.

Similarly to any other security protocol, Remark! is not designed to withstand every possible threat. For instance, it cannot cope with plagiarism but assumes appropriate invigilation during testing. Principals may still collude and communicate via subliminal channels, for example by using steganography. Although it is hard to rule out completely such a threat, steganalysis techniques can be of some help here. Other countermeasures may be needed against collusion attacks that exploit covert channels. We thus specify seven assumptions

© Springer International Publishing AG 2018
R. Giustolisi, *Modelling and Verification of Secure Exams*, Information Security and Cryptography, https://doi.org/10.1007/978-3-319-67107-9_5

conveniently for the goals of Remark!. In particular, we assume that:

1. Each principal holds a long-term public/private pair of keys.

2. The candidate holds a smart card in which the personal details of the candidate are visibly engraved. The smart card securely stores the candidate's private key, namely the private key cannot be extracted from the smart card.

3. The candidate is invigilated during testing to mitigate cheating. Invigilation for remote testing can be guaranteed with online invigilation software, such as ProctorU [Inc15].

4. The model answers are kept secret from the candidates until after testing. The examiners may be provided with the model answers at marking.

5. An authenticated append-only bulletin board that guarantees that everyone can see the same data is available, though write access might be restricted to appropriate entities [BRT13].

6. An implementation of TLS channel that ensures integrity and confidentiality of messages is available.

Outline of the chapter. Section 5.1 reviews a few proposals of secure protocols for Internet-based exams. Section 5.2 details the basics of exponentiation mixnet, the cryptographic scheme on which Remark! is based. Section 5.3 describes Remark! according to the four phases of an exam. Section 5.4 contains the formal analysis in ProVerif of authentication, privacy, and verifiability requirements. Finally, Section 5.5 discusses future work and concludes the chapter.

5.1 Internet-Based Exams

Internet-based exams are probably not the most practised type of exam, but they are becoming more popular in innovative educational test technologies. MOOC companies offer students Internet-based exams that grant them credits for many universities [Lew13]. TOEFL [TOE], which is one of the major English-language tests in the world, has replaced its traditional exams with Internet-based exams. However, to the best of our knowledge, neither the specification nor the security requirements of MOOCs and TOEFL protocols are publicly available. Moreover, their design probably includes a trusted exam authority that is in charge of the critical tasks of the exam. Conversely, Remark! is designed to minimise the reliance on trusted parties. Huszti-Pethő [HP10] advanced an Internet-based exam with a few trust requirements on principals, but in Chapter 3 we have shown that the protocol has several security issues. In contrast, we prove that Remark! ensures all the security requirements.

In the domain of Computer Supported Collaborative Working, Foley and Jacob [FJ95] formalised confidentiality requirements and proposed an exam as a case study. Maffei et al. [MPR13] implemented a course evaluation system that guarantees privacy using anonymous credential schemes without a trusted third party. Similarly, Hohenberger et al. [HMPs14] advanced *ANONIZE*, a protocol

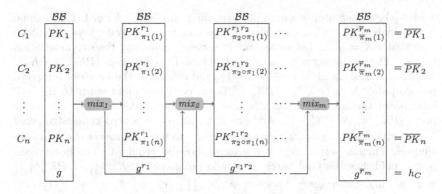

Figure 5.1: The exponentiation mixnet scheme

for surveys that ensures authentication and privacy in the presence of corrupted authorities. However, surveys have different security requirements than exams, for instance, surveys do not consider test authorship related requirements and fixed-term anonymity definitions.

Some protocols have been proposed in the area of conference management systems. Kanav *et al.* [KLP14] introduced *CoCon*, a formally verified implementation of a conference management system that guarantees confidentiality. Arapinis *et al.* [ABR12] introduced and formally analysed *ConfiChair*, a cryptographic protocol that addresses secrecy and privacy risks coming from a *malicious-but-cautious* cloud. Their work has been recently extended to support any cloud-based system that assumes honest managers, such as a public tender management and recruitment process [ABR13]. In Remark!, a different attacker is considered since exam authorities, which are analogous to managers in cloud-based systems, can be corrupted.

5.2 Exponentiation Mixnet

The design of Remark! relies on ElGamal encryption, digital signatures, and exponentiation mixnet. In this section, we detail the rudiments of exponentiation mixnet, while the reader can refer to Chapter 3 for a brief description of ElGamal encryption and digital signatures.

The main functionality provided by exponentiation mixnet is to generate a *pseudo* public key that allows the owner of the corresponding private key to encrypt and sign messages anonymously. An exponentiation mixnet takes in a batch of public keys and outputs a set of new pseudo public keys. The scheme ensures that no one but the owner of the public/private key pair can link a public key of the original batch with any of the pseudo public keys. In contrast to conventional re-encryption mixnet [Cha81] in which each term is independently re-encrypted, the peculiarity of exponentiation mixnet is that each mix server re-encrypts the terms by a common exponent value. This idea appeared first in the work of Haenni and Spycher [HS11]. In the following, we detail the construction of an exponentiation mixnet, which is depicted in Figure 5.1.

Let g be a generator of a multiplicative subgroup $\mathbb{G}$ of order q. Let us assume n principals $\langle C_1, \ldots C_n \rangle$, each having a pair of public/private keys (PK, SK) such that $PK = g^{SK}$. Let us assume m servers composing the exponentiation mixnet. The mix server mix_1 takes the batch of the public keys $\langle PK_1, \ldots PK_n \rangle$, generates a fresh random $r_1 \in \{1, q - 1\}$, and computes the batch of temporal pseudo public keys $\langle PK_1^{r_1}, \ldots PK_n^{r_1} \rangle$. Then, mix_1 signs and sends to the bulletin board the computed batch in a secret shuffled order, namely the server posts $\langle PK_{\overline{\pi}_1(1)}^{\overline{r}_1}, \ldots PK_{\overline{\pi}_1(n)}^{\overline{r}_1} \rangle$. Additionally, mix_1 posts a zero-knowledge proof of correctness and sends the new generator g^{r_1} to the next server over a secure channel. Further servers repeat the steps above as required. The last server, mix_m, publishes the final batch of pseudo public key $\langle PK_{\overline{\pi}_m(1)}^{\overline{r}_m}, \ldots PK_{\overline{\pi}_m(n)}^{\overline{r}_m} \rangle$ and the final generator $g^{\overline{r}_m}$, where $\overline{r}_m = \prod_{i=1}^m r_i$ and $\overline{\pi}_m = \pi_k \circ \cdots \circ \pi_1$. Note that the intermediate $g^{r_1}, \ldots, g^{\overline{r}_{m-1}}$ terms are not posted on the bulletin board. This prevents each principal to trace their intermediate pseudo public keys through the mixnet. Although it is not clear whether such eventuality is an attack, it is normally considered an undesired feature. Each principal C_i can find the corresponding pseudo public key using their private keys, since $g^{\overline{r}_m SK_i} = PK_{\overline{\pi}_m(i)}^{\overline{r}_m}$.

Remark! makes use of exponentiation mixnet at preparation to create the pseudonyms for candidates and examiners. The mixnet is also required at notification to revoke the pseudonyms of candidates. In so doing, each server mix_i reveals its random value r_i, hence by revealing all the values $\overline{r}_m$ it is possible to link the pseudonyms to the identities of the candidates.

5.3   Protocol Description

Remark! has four roles: exam authority (EA), candidate (C), examiner (E), and mixnet (NET). The exam authority manages the exam and also plays the roles of collector and notifier.

Remark! relies on a bulletin board to publish pseudonyms, questions, tests, and marks. As we discussed in the previous section, the bulletin board is also used in the exponentiation mixnet scheme. In the remainder, we assume that anyone can post messages on the bulletin board, even the attacker. Thus, we require each principal to sign their messages. However, if one assumes that the bulletin board has appropriate write access control mechanisms, namely it only publishes messages that originate from eligible principals, signatures may not be necessary. In the following, we detail Remark! according to the phases of an exam. Figure 5.2 illustrates the protocol's steps in form of a message sequence chart.

Preparation

The exponentiation mixnet generates the pseudonyms of candidate and examiner. The generation takes place in two independent runs: first the mixnet generates the pseudonym of candidates and then the pseudonym of examiners. Such separation is necessary because only the identities of candidates should be revealed at notification.

The public key PK_C of an eligible candidate C is processed by the exponentiation mixnet among the public keys of other candidates. After the last mix

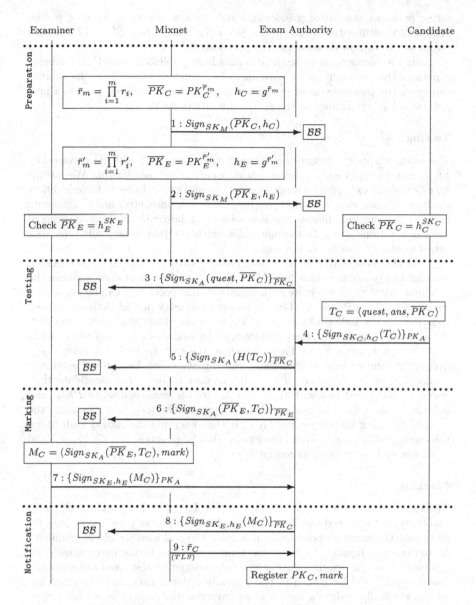

Figure 5.2: The Remark! Internet-based exam protocol

server publishes the list of pseudonyms and the new generator $h_C := g^{\bar{r}m}$, the candidate identifies her pseudo public key $\overline{PK}_C$ computing $h_C^{SK_C}$. The pseudo public key from now on serves as the pseudonym for C.

After the pseudonyms of candidates have been published (step 1), the mixnet generates the pseudonyms for examiners in a similar way. Since the mixnet generates the pseudonyms of examiners using different random values, a new generator h_E is published at the end of the mix (step 2).

Testing

The exam authority generates the questions, signs them with its private key SK_A, and encrypts each question under a candidate pseudonym. We do not specify how the exam authority generates the questions in order to include different forms of questions (e.g., multiple choice, free-response, etc.) and assignments (e.g., single question, different questions for candidate, random permutations of a set of questions, etc.). In the remainder, with *question* we actually refer to a list of questions possibly of size one.

Remark! assumes that an invigilator authenticates the candidate by checking whether the personal details printed on the top of the smart card matches the candidate identity. For remote authentication, this procedure can be supported with tools such as ProctorU. Then, the exam authority publishes the encrypted questions on the bulletin board (step 3). After the candidate answers the test, she appends the answer to her pseudonym and question, so the filled test consists of $T_C = \langle ques, ans, \overline{PK}_C \rangle$. Then, she signs the test T_C with her private key SK_C using the generator h_C. Thus, the signature can be verified using the pseudonym of the candidate $\overline{PK}_C$ with respect to h_C. The candidate then encrypts the signed test with the public key of the exam authority PK_A, and submits it (step 4). The exam authority decrypts the test, and then signs the hash of T_C using its private key SK_A. It then encrypts the signed hash under the corresponding candidate's pseudonym, that is, $\{Sign_{SK_A}(H(T_C))\}_{\overline{PK}_C}$, and publishes such encryption as receipt (step 5).

Marking

The exam authority randomly chooses an eligible examiner pseudonym $\overline{PK}_E$, and encrypts the signed test T_C under the chosen examiner pseudonym (step 6). Note that the exam authority does not know the real identity of the examiner. Moreover, it is possible to introduce a universally verifiable deterministic assignment of test to examiners. For example, encrypted tests and the examiner pseudonyms could be posted in two lexically ordered lists, and the exam authority cyclically assigns a test to an examiner according to the order.

After the designated examiner marks the test, he appends the mark to the signed test, thus generating the evaluation $M_C = \langle Sign_{SK_A}(\overline{PK}_E, T_C), mark \rangle$. The examiner then signs M_C with his private key SK_E and the generator h_E, and encrypts the signed evaluation under the public key of the exam authority PK_A (step 7).

Notification

The exam authority receives from the examiner the encrypted evaluation, which it decrypts and re-encrypts under the corresponding candidate pseudonym $\overline{PK}_C$.

After the exam authority publishes all the test evaluations (step 8), it asks
the mixnet to reveal the random values r used to generate the pseudonyms
of the candidates (step 9). In so doing, the candidate anonymity is revoked,
and the mark can finally be registered. Note that each candidate learns the
corresponding mark before $\bar{r}_m$ is revealed.

5.4   Security of Remark!

The security analysis of Remark! considers all the authentication, privacy, and
verifiability requirements formally specified in Chapter 3. A recall of the requirements with short informal descriptions is below:

- Authentication

  - *Candidate Authorisation*, which says that only registered candidates
    can take the exam.

  - *Answer Authenticity*, which says that the exam authority considers
    only the answers that candidates actually submitted.

  - *Test Origin Authentication*, which says that the exam authority ac-
    cepts only tests that originate from registered candidates.

  - *Test Authenticity*, which says that the examiner only marks the tests
    intended for him.

  - *Mark Authenticity*, which says that the exam authority stores the
    marks as assigned to the tests by the examiners.

  - *Mark Authentication*, which says that the candidate is notified with
    the mark stored by the exam authority.

- Privacy

  - *Question Indistinguishability*, which says that the questions are not
    revealed until testing begins.

  - *Anonymous Marking*, which says that the examiner marks a test
    while ignoring its author.

  - *Anonymous Examiner*, which says that the candidate cannot learn
    which examiner marked her test.

  - *Mark Privacy*, which says that no one learns the marks, besides the
    examiner, the concerned candidate, and the exam authority.

  - *Mark Anonymity*, which says that no one learns the association be-
    tween a mark and the corresponding candidate, besides the concerned
    candidate, and the exam authority.

- Individual Verifiability: a candidate can check that

  - *Question Validity*: she received the questions actually generated by
    the exam authority.

  - *Marking Correctness*: the mark she received is correctly computed
    on her test.

  - *Test Integrity*: her test is accepted and marked as she submitted it.

Primitive	Equation
ElGamal encryption	$decrypt(encrypt(m, pk(k), r), k) = m$ $decrypt(encrypt(m, pseudo\_pub(pk(k)),$ $rce), r), pseudo\_priv(k, exp(rce))) = m$ $checkpseudo(pseudo\_pub(pk(k), rce),$ $pseudo\_priv(k, exp(rce))) = true$
Digital signature	$getmess(sign(m, k)) = m$ $checksign(sign(m, k), spk(k)) = m$ $checksign(sign(m, pseudo\_priv(k,$ $exp(rce))), pseudo\_pub(pk(k), rce)) = m$

Table 5.1: Equational theory to model Remark!

- *Test Markedness*: the test she submitted is marked without modification.

- *Marking Integrity*: the mark attributed to her test is assigned to her without any modification.

- *Marking Notification*: she received the mark assigned to her.

• Universal Verifiability: an auditor can check that

- *Registration*: all accepted tests are submitted by registered candidates.

- *Marking Correctness*: all the marks attributed by the examiners to the tests are computed correctly.

- *Test Integrity*: all and only accepted tests are marked without any modification.

- *Test Markedness*: only the accepted tests are marked without modification.

- *Marking Integrity*: all and only the marks associated to the tests are assigned to the corresponding candidates with no modifications.

Model Choices

We analyse Remark! in ProVerif. The equational theory is depicted in Table 5.1. The theory consists of the standard equations for ElGamal encryption and digital signatures extended with novel equations that model pseudonyms as public keys. The pseudonym, which also serves as test identifier, can be generated using the function *pseudo_pub*, which takes in a public key and a random exponent. In fact, this function models the main feature of exponentiation mixnet. The function *pseudo_priv* can be used by a principal to decrypt or sign anonymous messages. The function takes in the private key of the principal and the new generator published by the mixnet. The function *checkpseudo* allows a principal to check whether a pseudonym is associated with the principal's private key. In practice, principals use this function to identify their pseudonyms published on the bulletin board. A public channel models the bulletin board.

```
let EA (skA:skey, pkN:pkey, ques:bitstring) =
(*Preparation*)
 in(bbn, (pseudo_C:pkey, hc:bitstring, r: role, spseC:bitstring));
 if (pseudo_C, hc, r) = checksign(spseC, pkN) && r = C then
  let sques = sign(ques, skA) in
  let eques = encrypt( (ques,sques), pseudo_C) in
  out(bba, eques);
  in(ch, eca:bitstring);
  let ((=ques, ans:bitstring, =pseudo_C), sca:bitstring) =
  decrypt(eca, skA) in
  if (ques, ans, pseudo_C) = checksign(sca, pseudo_C) then
   (* EA collects the test from C with pseudonym pseudo_C *)
   event collected(pseudo_C, ques, ans);
   let ca = (ques, ans, pseudo_C) in
   let sca' = sign(ca, skA)  in
   let eca' = encrypt((ca, sca'), pseudo_C) in
   out(bba, eca');

(* Marking *)
   in(bbn, (pseudo_E:pkey, he:bitstring, rolet:role,
     spseE:bitstring));
   if (pseudo_E, he, rolet) = checksign(spseE, pkN) &&
     rolet = E then
   let ca'' = (ques, ans, pseudo_C, pseudo_E) in
   let sca'' = sign(ca'', skA)  in
   let eca'' = encrypt((ca'', sca''), pseudo_E) in
   (* EA distributed the test (pseudo_C,ques,ans) *)
   (* identified by pseudo_C (id_form = pseudo_C) to E pseudo_E*)
   event distributed(pseudo_C,ques,ans,pseudo_C,pseudo_E);
   out(bba, eca'');
   in(ch, ema:bitstring);
   let ((=ca'', =sca'', mark:bitstring), sma:bitstring) =
   decrypt(ema, skA) in
   if (ca'', sca'', mark) = checksign(sma, pseudo_E)  then

(* Notification *)
    let ma = (ca'', sca'', mark) in
    let ema' = encrypt((ma, sma), pseudo_C) in
    out(bba, ema');
    (*Reveal ID*)
    in(ch, encsignetX: bitstring).
```

Figure 5.3: The process of the exam authority

```
let Cand (skC:skey, pkA:pkey, pkN:pkey, ans:bitstring) =
(*Preparation *)
 in(bbn, (pseudo_C:pkey, hc:bitstring, r: role, spseC:bitstring));
 if (pseudo_C, hc, r) = checksign(spseC, pkN) && r = C then
  let priv_C = pseudo_priv(skC, hc) in
  if checkpseudo(pseudo_C, priv_C) =true then

(*Testing*)
  in(bba, eques:bitstring);
  let (ques: bitstring, sques:bitstring)=decrypt(eques, priv_C) in
  if ques=checksign(sques, pkA) then
   let ca = (ques, ans, pseudo_C) in
   let sca = sign(ca,priv_C) in
   let eca = encrypt((ca, sca), pkA) in
   (* C with pseudo_C  submits his test (ques, ans) *)
   event submitted(pseudo_C, ques, ans);
   out(ch, eca);
   in(bba, eca':bitstring);
   let (=ca, sca':bitstring) = decrypt(eca', priv_C) in
   if (ques, ans, pseudo_C) = checksign(sca', pkA) then

(*Notification*)
    in(bba, ema':bitstring);
    in(bbn, (pseudo_E:pkey, he:bitstring, role_E: role,
       spseE:bitstring));
    if (pseudo_E, he, E) = checksign(spseE, pkN) then
     let ((ca'': bitstring, sca'': bitstring, mark:bitstring),
          sma:bitstring) = decrypt(ema', priv_C) in
      if ca''=(ques, ans, pseudo_C, pseudo_E) &&
         ca''=checksign(sca'', pkA) then
       if ((ques, ans, pseudo_C, pseudo_E), sca'', mark) =
          checksign(sma, pseudo_E) then
        (* C with pseudo_C is notified with "mark" *)
        event notified(pseudo_C, mark).
```

Figure 5.4: The process of the candidate

```
let NET (skN:skey, pkA:pkey, rc:bitstring) =
 in(ch, (R: role));
 get publickey(=R, rx, pkX) in
 let hx = exp(rx) in
 let pseudo_X = pseudo_pub(pkX,rx) in
 let spseX = sign ((pseudo_X, hx, R), skN) in
 out(bbn, ( pseudo_X, hx, R, spseX));
 (*Reveal rc*)
 let signetX = sign( (rc), skN) in
 let encsignetX = encrypt ( (rc, signetX), pkA) in
 out(ch, encsignetX).
```

Figure 5.5: The process of the mixnet

```
let Ex (skE:skey, pkA:pkey, pkN:pkey, mark:bitstring) =
(*Preparation *)
 in(bbn, (pseudo_E:pkey, he:bitstring, r: role, spseE:bitstring));
 if (pseudo_E, he, E) = checksign(spseE, pkN) then
  let priv_E = pseudo_priv(skE, he) in
  if checkpseudo(pseudo_E, priv_E) =true then

(* Marking *)
  in(bba, eca'':bitstring);
  let ((ques:bitstring, ans:bitstring, pseudo_C:pkey, =pseudo_E),
      sca':bitstring) = decrypt(eca'', priv_E) in
  if (ques, ans, pseudo_C,pseudo_E) = checksign(sca', pkA) then
   let ca = (ques, ans, pseudo_C, pseudo_E) in
   let ma:bitstring = (ca, sca', mark) in
   let sma:bitstring = sign(ma,priv_E) in
   let ema = encrypt((ma, sma), pkA) in
   event marked(ques,ans,mark,pseudo_C,pseudo_E);
   (* E with  pseudo_E marked the test (ques, ans) *)
   (* identified by pseudo_C with mark *)
   out(ch, ema).
```

Figure 5.6: The process of the examiner

```
process
 !(
 (*Products of the secret exponent values of the servers *)
 (* (represented by the NET): rc for C and re for E *)
 new rc: bitstring;
 new re: bitstring;
 (*Assume one NET and one EA*)
 new skA: skey; let pkA = pk(skA) in out (ch, pkA);
 new skN: skey; let pkN = pk(skN) in out (ch, pkN);

 (!( NET(skN, pkA, rc))) |
 (!( new ques:bitstring;  EA(skA, pkN, ques))) |
 (!( new skC: skey; let pkC = pk(skC) in out (ch, pkC);
     new ans:bitstring; insert publickey(C, rc, pkC);
     Cand(skC, pkA, pkN, ans))
   ) |
 (!( new skE: skey; let pkE = pk(skE) in out (ch, pkE);
     new mark:bitstring; insert publickey(E, re, pkE);
     Ex(skE, pkA, pkN, mark))
   )

)
```

Figure 5.7: The exam process

Requirement	Result	Time	Honest roles
Candidate Authorisation	✓	1 s	(C, EA, NET)
Answer Authenticity	✓	1 s	(E, EA, NET)
Test Origin Authentication	✓	1 s	(NET)
Test Authenticity	✓	1 s	(E, EA, NET)
Mark Authenticity	✓	1 s	(E, EA, NET)
Question Indistinguishability	✓	1 s	(E, EA, NET)
Anonymous Marking	✓	1 s	(C, NET)
Anonymous Examiner	✓	1 s	(E, NET)
Mark Privacy	✓	3 m 39 s	(EA, NET)

Table 5.2: Summary of authentication and privacy analysis of Remark!

Authentication and Privacy

The process of the exam authority is in Figure 5.3, the process of the mixnet is in Figure 5.5, the process of the candidate is in Figure 5.4, and the process of examiner is in Figure 5.6. The exam process is depicted in Figure 5.7. In each process we replace the identity of candidate with the corresponding candidate's pseudonym inside the events. This choice is sound because the equational theory preserves the bijective mapping between keys and pseudonyms.

We check authentication and privacy in ProVerif with the same approach used in Chapter 3 to verify the Huszti-Pethő protocol. In particular, we use ProVerif's `noninterf` and `choice[]` commands to verify the privacy requirements. The full ProVerif code is available upon request from the author.

Results. Assuming an attacker in control of the network and honest principals, ProVerif successfully proves all authentication and privacy requirements. Table 5.2 reports the execution times over an Intel Core i7 3.0 GHz machine with 8 GB RAM. Also assuming corrupted principals, ProVerif proves that Remark! ensures all the requirements. Table 5.2 also reports the honest roles that are required for each requirement to hold. Note that only the processes needed to specify the requirement are modelled. For example, the specification of Anonymous Marking requires two candidates to be honest, otherwise they could just reveal their tests to the attacker, who would trivially be able to violate the protocol. However, all other candidates can be corrupted and collude with the attacker to violate the protocol.

Notably, Remark! ensures a stronger version of Anonymous Examiner since no one, even the exam authority, knows which examiner marks which test. It can be observed that Mark Anonymity is not in Figure 5.2: since Remark! ensures Mark Privacy, it also guarantees Mark Anonymity.

Remark. We report an issue on an early version of Remark! that witnesses how formal approaches contribute to achieve a deep understanding of the design models. In the first draft of Remark!, the receipt of submission of a test T_C consisted of the message $\{Sign_{SK_A}(T_C)\}_{\overline{PK}_C}$, that is, the exam authority signs the test and posts the signed test encrypted with the candidate's pseudonym. Moreover, the assignment of the test to the examiner consisted of the message

$\{Sign_{SK_A}(T_C)\}_{\overline{PK_E}}$, namely the signed test encrypted with an eligible examiner's pseudonym. The rest of the protocol was unchanged respect to the current version. With these two modifications ProVerif cannot prove Test Authenticity. In fact, the attack trace shows that a corrupted candidate can pick an examiner of her choice by re-encrypting the signed receipt received from the exam authority. It means that the candidate can influence the choice of the examiner who marks her test. Such attack could be avoided assuming an access control mechanism that would not allow the candidate to post on the bulletin board.

However, the fixes implemented in the final version of Remark! shows that there is no need for access control mechanisms to secure the protocol. The first fix consists in signing the hash of the test as receipt. The second fix consists in making the pseudonym of the chosen examiner explicit. In doing so, the signature of the exam authority within the receipt cannot be used by a candidate to designate any examiner.

Verifiability

The ProVerif model proposed to check authentication and privacy in the previous section can be also used to analyse Remark! for verifiability. The definitions of authentication and privacy introduced in Chapter 3 are formulated in the applied π-calculus and can be coded straight to ProVerif. Conversely, verifiability definitions are expressed in a more abstract model. Thus, it is necessary to map sets and relations specified in the verifiability model to Remark!.

We recall that Definition 29, which we introduced in Chapter 3, considers the data sets I, Q, A, M, and their elements i, q, a, m, which specify the candidate identities, the questions, the answers, and the marks respectively. In Remark!, the set I contains the candidate pseudonyms rather than the identities. In the previous section we argued this choice to be sound. The sets Q, A, and M contains the messages that correspond to questions, answers and marks generated by the protocol's principals, possibly manipulated by the attacker.

The relations Accepted, Marked, and Assigned are built from the posts that appear on the bulletin board. The tuples $(i, (q, a))$ of the relation Accepted consist of the receipts of submission that the exam authority publishes on the bulletin board at the end of testing. The tuples $(i, (q, a), m)$ of the relation Marked coincide with the tuples (i, m) of Assigned, and consist of the messages that the exam authority publishes on the bulletin board at marking. Precisely, the tuples $(i, (q, a), m)$ are generated from the marked test signed by the examiner, that is, $Sign_{SK_E, h_E}(M_C)$. The tuples (i, m) instead are built from the encryption of the marked test generated by the exam authority, that is, $\{Sign_{SK_E, h_E}(M_C)\}_{\overline{PK_C}}$. It can be observed that encryption under the candidate's pseudonym officially assigns the mark to the candidate.

Finally, the function Correct, which is the algorithm used to mark the tests, can be modelled as a ProVerif table.

Individual verifiability definitions require the existence of verifiability-tests that candidates run to check the properties of the protocol. We show that Remark! has the necessary verifiability-tests. In ProVerif, we model the verifiability-tests as processes that emit the event OK when the verifiability-test succeeds, and emit the event KO when the verifiability-test fails.

We use correspondence assertions to prove soundness. ProVerif checks verifiability as a reachability property. The verification strategy normally consists of checking that the event OK is always preceded by the event emitted in the part of the code where the predicate becomes satisfied. In the ProVerif model of Remark! we assume an honest candidate principal who plays the role of the verifier. The other principals are usually corrupted, if not stated otherwise. The verifiability-test receives the data from the candidate via a private channel, and the remaining data posted on the bulletin board via public channels. This allows an attacker to manipulate the input data. Corrupted principals may collude with the attacker.

We resort to unreachability of the event KO to prove completeness. In this case, the ProVerif model enforces only honest principals and prevents the attacker to manipulate the input data of the verifiability-tests. In fact, a complete verifiability-test must succeed if its input data is correct.

In the following paragraphs, we specify the verifiability-tests for Remark!. We also discuss the conditions to achieve sound and complete verifiability-tests according to each individual verifiability requirement.

Question Validity. Remark! assumes that the exam authority generates the questions at preparation and publishes them at testing. Thus, we model the exam authority as an honest process in ProVerif, otherwise a corrupted exam authority would publish questions that are different from the ones actually generated.

The verifiability-test *testQV*, which is depicted in Figure 5.8, receives the question *eques* that is published on the bulletin board from a public channel. It also receives the candidate's question *ques* and private key *priv_C* from a private channel. The verifiability-test checks whether the candidate actually received the question published by the exam authority on the bulletin board.

To prove soundness, we annotate the ProVerif process of the exam authority with the event **generated** where the questions are generated. Then, ProVerif checks if the verifiability-test emits the event OK only if the exam authority actually generated the question received from the candidate, namely ProVerif checks the following correspondence assertion:

$$\text{OK}\langle ques \rangle \rightsquigarrow \text{generated}\langle ques \rangle$$

To prove completeness, ProVerif checks that the verifiability-test process does not emit the event KO when the input data is correct. ProVerif confirms the verifiability-test is sound and complete, so we can conclude that Remark! is question validity verifiable.

Marking Correctness. Remark! is designed to support different forms of questions (e.g., multiple choice, free-response, etc.), hence there is no universal marking algorithm that can be used to evaluate the answers. However, we can assume that the exam authority publishes the table of evaluations that maps an answer to a mark after the exam concludes. We thus model the exam authority as an honest process in ProVerif to check Marking Correctness.

The verifiability-test *testMC*, which is in Figure 5.9, receives the test (*ques*, *ans*) submitted by the candidate, and the mark *mark* notified to her. The verifiability-test checks if the mark reported on the table of evaluations and associated to the candidate's answer coincides with the mark received from the candidate.

```
let testQV(pkA: pkey, pch: channel) =
 in(bba, eques:bitstring);
 in(pch, (ques: bitstring, priv_C: skey));

 let (ques':bitstring, sques:bitstring) =
     decrypt(eques, priv_C) in
 let (ques'':bitstring,p seudoC:bitstring) =
     checksign(sques, pkA) in

 if ques'=ques && ques''=ques' then event OK
 else event KO.
```

Figure 5.8: The Question Validity individual verifiability-test

```
let testMC (pkA: pkey, priv_ch: channel) =
 in(priv_ch, (ques: bitstring, ans: bitstring, mark: bitstring));

 get correct_ans(=ques,=ans,mark':bitstring) in

 if mark'=mark then
  event OK
 else KO.
```

Figure 5.9: The Marking Correctness individual verifiability-test

To prove soundness, we annotate the ProVerif process of the candidate with the event **correct** where the candidate receives the mark at notification. ProVerif checks that if the verifiability-test emits the event OK, then a previous event **correct** was emitted. This is formalised as:

$$\text{OK}\langle ques, ans, mark \rangle \rightsquigarrow \text{correct}\langle ques, ans, mark \rangle$$

ProVerif checks that the verifiability-test does not emit the event KO to prove completeness.

Thus, assuming an honest exam authority that provides the table of evaluations at end of exam, Remark! is marking correctness verifiable.

Test Integrity. The verifiability-test *testTI* in Figure 5.10 takes in the test (*ques,ans*) submitted by the candidate via a private channel, and the receipt of submission *eca'* and the notification *ema'* published on the bulletin board via a public channel. The verifiability-test checks if candidate's submission, the receipt, and the notification contain the same question, answer, and pseudonym.

To prove soundness, we annotate the verifiability-test with the events **accepted** and **marked** that map the corresponding relations. In particular, the receipt of submission is part of the relation **Accepted** if it is signed by the exam authority and encrypted under the pseudonym of the candidate. Similarly, the notification is part of the relation **Marked** if it is signed by the examiner and

```
let testTI (pkA: pkey, priv_ch: channel) =
 in(priv_ch, (priv_C: skey, ques: bitstring, ans: bitstring,
              pseudo_C: pkey));
 in(bbn, (pseudo_E:pkey, he:bitstring, rolet: role,
        spseE:bitstring));
 in(bba, eca': bitstring);
 in(bba, ema':bitstring);

 (* If the message on the BB is signed by the authority, *)
 (* it is considered as part of the relation Accepted. *)
 let (ca: bitstring, sca':bitstring) = decrypt(eca', priv_C) in
 let (ques': bitstring, ans': bitstring, pseudo_C': pkey) =
     checksign(sca', pkA) in
 (* If the message on the BB is signed by the examiner, *)
 (* it is considered as part of the relation Marked. *)
 let (((ques'': bitstring, ans'': bitstring, pseudo_C'': pkey),
       sca1: bitstring, mark:bitstring), sma:bitstring) =
     decrypt(ema', priv_C) in
 let ((ques''': bitstring, ans''': bitstring, pseudo_C''': pkey),
       sca1': bitstring, mark':bitstring) =
     checksign(sma, pseudo_E) in

 if ques'=ques && ans'=ans && pseudo_C'=pseudo_C && ques''=ques &&
    ans''=ans && pseudo_C''=pseudo_C && (ques', ans', pseudo_C') =
    checksign(sca1,pkA) && ques'''=ques && ans'''=ans &&
    pseudo_C'''=pseudo_C && sca1'=sca1 then
  event OK
 else event KO.
```

Figure 5.10: The Test Integrity individual verifiability-test

```
let testTM (pkA: pkey, priv_ch: channel) =
 in(priv_ch, (priv_C: skey,ques: bitstring, ans: bitstring,
             pseudo_C: pkey));
 in(bbn, (pseudo_E:pkey, he:bitstring, rolet: role,
         spseE:bitstring));
 in(bba, ema:bitstring);

(* If the message on the BB is signed by the examiner, *)
(* it is considered as part of the relation Marked. *)
let (((ques': bitstring, ans': bitstring, pseudo_C': pkey),
      sca1: bitstring, mark:bitstring), sma:bitstring) =
    decrypt(ema, priv_C) in
let ((ques'': bitstring, ans'': bitstring, pseudo_C'': pkey),
     sca1': bitstring, mark':bitstring) =
    checksign(sma, pseudo_E) in

if ques'=ques && ans'=ans && pseudo_C'=pseudo_C &&ques''= ques &&
   ans''=ans && pseudo_C''=pseudo_C && (ques', ans', pseudo_C') =
   checksign(sca1,pkA) && sca1'=sca1 then
  event OK
else event KO.
```

Figure 5.11: The Test Markedness individual verifiability-test

encrypted under the pseudonym of the candidate. The requirement can be formalised with the following correspondence assertion:

$$\text{OK}\langle id, ques, ans \rangle \rightsquigarrow \text{marked}\langle id, ques, ans \rangle \cup \text{accepted}\langle id, ques, ans \rangle$$

To prove completeness, ProVerif checks that the verifiability-test process does not emit the event KO when the input data is correct.

ProVerif shows that the verifiability-test for Test Integrity is sound and complete. Note that a corrupted exam authority can publish two different receipts for the same test on the bulletin board. However, since the bulletin board is append-only, the candidate notices if the exam authority appends two different receipts for her submission because only the candidate knows the private key.

Test Markedness. Since Remark! has a sound and complete verifiability-test for Test Integrity, we can build from this a sound and complete verifiability-test for Test Markedness. It is sufficient to not consider the receipt of submission as input, and just check whether the candidate's submission and the data obtained from notification contain the same question, answer, and pseudonym. The verifiability-test *testTM* is depicted in Figure 5.11. To prove soundness, it is sufficient to prove the following correspondence assertion:

$$\text{OK}\langle id, ques, ans \rangle \rightsquigarrow \text{marked}\langle id, ques, ans \rangle$$

```
let testMI (pkA: pkey, priv_ch: channel) =
 in(priv_ch, (priv_C: skey,ques: bitstring, ans: bitstring,
    pseudo_C: pkey));
 in(bbn, (pseudo_E:pkey, he:bitstring, rolet: role,
    spseE:bitstring));
 in(bba, ema':bitstring);

(* Assigned is the mark sent by the authority *)
let (((ques': bitstring, ans': bitstring, pseudo_C': pkey),
      sca': bitstring, mark:bitstring), sma:bitstring) =
    decrypt(ema', priv_C) in
(* Marked are the marks signed by the examiner *)
let ((ques'': bitstring, ans'': bitstring, pseudo_C'': pkey),
     sca'': bitstring, mark': bitstring) =
    checksign(sma, pseudo_E) in

if ques'=ques && ans'=ans && pseudo_C'=pseudo_C && ques''=ques &&
   ans''=ans && pseudo_C''=pseudo_C && mark=mark' &&
   (ques', ans', pseudo_C')=checksign(sca',pkA) then
 event OK
else KO.
```

Figure 5.12: The Mark Integrity individual verifiability-test

Mark Integrity. The verifiability-test *testMI* in Figure 5.12 takes in the test ($ques, ans$) submitted by the candidate via a private channel, and the notification *ema'* published by the exam authority on the bulletin board. The verifiability-test checks if the test provided by the candidate and the notification on the bulletin board contain the same question, answer, and pseudonym, and if the examiner's signature on the mark is correct.

To check soundness in ProVerif, we annotate the verifiability-test with the events **assigned** and **marked** that map the corresponding relations. The data on the notification message is part of the relation **Assigned** if the data is signed by the exam authority and encrypted under the pseudonym of the candidate. This data is also part of the relation **Marked** if it also include the signature of the examiner. The correspondence assertion to check soundness is:

$$\text{OK}\langle id, ques, ans, mark\rangle \rightsquigarrow \text{marked}\langle id, ques, ans, mark\rangle \cup$$
$$\text{assigned}\langle id, ques, ans, mark\rangle$$

We check completeness as usual, and ProVerif confirms that the verifiability-test for Mark Integrity is sound and complete.

Mark Notification Integrity. The last individual verifiability definition concerns the check of the integrity of the notified mark. The verifiability-test *testMNI* in Figure 5.13 is fed via a private channel with the mark *mark* that the candidate received at notification. The verifiability-test *testMNI* also takes in the official notification *ema'* published in the bulletin board via a public chan-

```
let testMNI (pkA: pkey, priv_ch: channel) =
 in(priv_ch, (priv_C: skey,mark: bitstring, pseudo_C: pkey,
             ema': bitstring));
 in(bba, ema: bitstring);

 (* Assigned is the mark sent by the authority *)
 let (((ques:bitstring, ans: bitstring, pseudo_C':pkey),
      sca: bitstring, mark':bitstring), sma:bitstring) =
    decrypt(ema, priv_C) in

 if (ques,ans,pseudo_C')=checksign(sca, pkA) &&
    pseudo_C'=pseudo_C &&  mark'=mark then
  event OK
 else event KO.
```

Figure 5.13: The Mark Notification Integrity individual verifiability-test

Requirement	Soundness	Completeness
Question Validity	✓ (EA)	✓(all)
Test Integrity	✓	✓(all)
Test Markedness	✓	✓(all)
Marking Correctness	✓ (EA)	✓(all)
Mark Integrity	✓	✓(all)
Mark Notification Integrity	✓	✓(all)

Table 5.3: Summary of the analysis of Remark! for I.V. requirements

nel, and checks if the mark provided in the notification coincides with the one received from the candidate.

Similarly to Mark Integrity, we annotate the verifiability-test *testMNI* with the event **assigned** to prove soundness. ProVerif checks if the verifiability-test emits the event OK only if the mark notified to the candidate is the same officially assigned at the end of the exam. This is formalised as:

$$\text{OK}\langle id, mark \rangle \rightsquigarrow \text{assigned}\langle id, mark \rangle$$

Also in this case ProVerif checks that the verifiability-test process does not emit the event KO when the input data is correct to prove completeness. ProVerif confirms the verifiability-test is sound and complete, hence Remark! is mark notification integrity verifiable.

Table 5.3 summarises the results of the individual verifiability analysis of Remark! and reports the roles required to be honest.

Universal Verifiability

Also for the specification of universal verifiability definitions, we model verifiability-tests as processes that emit the event OK when the verifiability-test succeeds, and emit the event KO when the verifiability-test fails.

In the case of universal verifiability an auditor runs the verifiability-tests, namely the auditor plays the role of the verifier. This requires a different approach to prove soundness compared to the approach used for individual verifiability definitions, in which the candidate plays as verifier. In fact, in the case of universal verifiability also the candidate can be corrupted, hence it can be hard to find a ProVerif process that can be annotated with events to check soundness via correspondence assertions.

The different approach consists of proving soundness of the verifiability-tests using unreachability of the event KO. The underlying idea is that every time the verifiability-test succeeds, which means that it emits the event OK, we check if the decryption of the concerned ciphertext gives the expected plaintext. If not, the event KO is emitted, thus the verifiability-test is not sound.

As we shall see later, it is however possible to prove the soundness of the verifiability-test for Registration requirement using correspondence assertions. This is possible because the NET is assumed to be honest, hence the corresponding ProVerif process can be annotated with an event that is emitted when registration concludes. We always use unreachability of the event KO to prove completeness of the verifiability-tests.

Remark.   It can be noted that all messages posted by the exam authority on the bulletin board are encrypted under the pseudonym of either the candidate or the examiner, hence no public data can be used as it is by the auditor. Candidates and examiners hold long-term pairs of public/private keys, and it is implausible that they reveal their private keys for audit purposes. Since the auditor cannot decrypt a ciphertext message posted on the bulletin board, the auditor should be rather provided with the corresponding plaintext and pseudonym. In so doing, the auditor can encrypt the plaintext with the pseudonym and check if the encryption coincides with the same ciphertext message posted on the bulletin board. Since Remark! uses ElGamal encryption, which is probabilistic, the auditor should be also provided with the random value used to encrypt a message.

In the following, we specify the data that the exam authority should provide to the auditor after the exam concludes.

- Registration: the exam authority reveals the signatures inside the receipts $receipt = \{Sign_{SK_A}(H(T_C))\}_{\overline{PK}_C}$ posted on the bulletin board and the random values used to encrypt the receipts.

- Marking Correctness: the exam authority reveals the marked tests inside the evaluations $sma = \{Sign_{SK_E,h_E}(M_C)\}_{PK_A}$, the random values used to encrypt the marked tests, and the table *correct_ans* that maps each mark to each answer.

- Test Integrity: the exam authority reveals the marked tests inside the evaluations, the random values used to encrypt the marked tests, plus the data disclosed for Registration.

- Test Markedness: the exam authority reveals the same data disclosed for Test Integrity.

- Mark Integrity: the exam authority reveals the examiners' signatures on the marked tests inside the evaluations, and the random values used to encrypt the notifications $notif = \{Sign_{SK_E, h_E}(M_C)\}_{\overline{PK}_C}$ before posting them on the bulletin board.

We anticipate that it is not possible to automatically prove the universal verifiability requirements in ProVerif. To prove such requirements it is needed to iterate over all candidates, but ProVerif does not support loops. We thus prove the base case of each requirement automatically in ProVerif, in which it is considered only one accepted test or one assigned mark. Then, we provide manual induction proofs that generalise the ProVerif result to the general case with an arbitrary number of candidates.

Registration. The verifiability-test $testUR$, which is depicted in Figure 5.14, takes in from the bulletin board the pseudonyms of the candidates signed by the mixnet and the receipts of submissions generated by the exam authority. In so doing, the auditor can check that the exam authority accepted only tests signed with pseudonyms posted by the mixnet during preparation.

ProVerif proves that the verifiability-test is complete and sound for the base case, which considers one accepted test and an unbounded number of candidates. To prove the general case, namely for an unbounded number of accepted tests and candidates, it is necessary to show that

$$testUR(E) = true \Leftrightarrow \{i : (i, x) \in \texttt{Accepted}\} \subseteq I_r$$

holds for an exam execution E that considers any size n of the relation $\texttt{Accepted}$ and any number m of registered candidates.

Let $testUR_k(\cdot)$ be the verifiability-test applied to an exam execution that has k accepted tests; let $testUR_k(\cdot) \rightarrow^* OK$ denote the verifiability-test that outputs OK (true) after some steps; let E be an exam execution that has m registered candidates and n accepted tests; let E_j be a version of E that only considers the jth accepted test, which is submitted by the candidate i_j. Since ProVerif proves that the verifiability-test is complete and sound for one accepted test and any number of registered candidates, it follows that for soundness we have

$$\forall 1 \leq j \leq n : testUR_1(E_j) \rightarrow^* OK \Rightarrow i_j \in I_r$$

and for completeness we have

$$\forall 1 \leq j \leq n : i_j \in I_r \Rightarrow testUR_1(E_j) \rightarrow^* OK.$$

The verifiability-test $testUR_n(E)$ checks if each of the accepted tests received on channels bba1, ..., bban was submitted by one of the candidates given on channels bbn1, ..., bbnn. The verifiability-test $\forall 1 \leq j \leq n : testUR_1(E_j)$ checks if the jth accepted test received on the channel bbaj was submitted by one of the candidates given on the channels bbn1, ..., bbnn.

We have that

$$testUR_n(E) \rightarrow^* OK$$
$$\Downarrow$$
$$\forall 1 \leq j \leq n : testUR_1(E_j) \rightarrow^* OK$$
$$\Downarrow_{(by\ ProVerif)}$$
$$\forall 1 \leq j \leq n : i_j \in I_r$$

```
let testUR(pkN, pkA, ch1,...,chn, bbn1,...,bbnm, bba1,...,bban)=
 in(bbn1, (pseudo_C1, hc, r, NET_sign1));
 ...
 in(bbnm, (pseudo_Cm, hc, r, NET_signm));

 in(bba1, receipt1);
 ...
 in(bban, receiptn);

 in(ch1, (rcoin1, EA_sign_rcpt1));
 ...
 in(chn, (rcoinn, EA_sign_rcptn));

 let (quest1, answ1, pseudo_C'1) =
 checksign(EA_sign_rcpt1, pkA) in
 ...
 let (questn, answn, pseudo_C'n) =
 checksign(EA_sign_rcptn, pkA) in

 (* If the pseudonym on the BB is signed by the NET, *)
 (* it is considered as part of the relation Accepted. *)
 if (pseudo_C1, hc, r)=checksign(NET_sign1, pkN) && r=C &&
    pseudo_C1=pseudo_C'1
    ||...||
    (pseudo_C1, hc, r)=checksign(NET_sign1, pkN) && r=C &&
    pseudo_C1=pseudo_C'n
    &&...&&
    (pseudo_Cm, hc, r)=checksign(NET_signm, pkN) && r=C &&
    pseudo_Cm=pseudo_C'1
    ||...||
    (pseudo_Cm, hc, r)=checksign(NET_signm, pkN) && r=C &&
    pseudo_Cm=pseudo_C'n   then
  if receipt1=int_encrypt(((quest1, answ1, pseudo_C'1),
                           EA_sign_rcpt1), pseudo_C1, rcoin1)
    &&...&&
    receiptn=int_encrypt(((questn, answn, pseudo_C'n),
                           EA_sign_rcptn), pseudo_Cm, rcoinn)
 then event OK
 else event KO
else event KO.
```

Figure 5.14: The Registration universal verifiability-test

$$\Downarrow$$
$$\{i : (i, x) \in \text{Accepted}\} \subseteq I_r$$

Thus, the verifiability-test *testUR* is sound also for the general case.

$$\{i : (i, x) \in \text{Accepted}\} \subseteq I_r$$
$$\Downarrow$$
$$\forall 1 \leq j \leq n : i_j \in I_r$$
$$\Downarrow_{(by\ ProVerif)}$$
$$\forall 1 \leq j \leq n : testUR_1(E_j) \rightarrow^* OK$$
$$\Downarrow$$
$$testUR_n(E) \rightarrow^* OK$$

Also the verifiability-test *testUR* is complete for the general case.

Marking Correctness. The verifiability-test *testUMC*, which is depicted in Figure 5.15, takes as input from the bulletin board the pseudonym of the examiner signed by the mixnet, and the mark notifications signed by the examiner and published by the exam authority. The auditor can obtain the evaluations generated by the examiner from the mark notifications. Then, the auditor checks if the mark assigned to the question of each test coincides with the mark associated to the same question on the table provided by the exam authority. Remark! intuitively ensures this requirement only if the exam authority is honest as it provides the table at the conclusion of the exam. For simplicity, we assume that one examiner marks all the tests.

ProVerif proves soundness and completeness of the verifiability-test assuming only one marked test, namely the relation Marked has only one entry. To prove the general case, we should consider an unbounded number of marked test. Thus, it is necessary to show that

$$testUMC(E) = true \Leftrightarrow \forall (i, x, m) \in \text{Marked}, \text{Correct}(x) = m$$

holds for an exam execution E that considers any size n of the relation Marked.

Let $MC_k(\cdot)$ be the verifiability-test applied to an exam execution that has k marked tests; let $MC_k(\cdot) \rightarrow^* OK$ denote the verifiability-test that outputs OK (true) after some steps; let E be an exam execution that has n marked tests; let E_j be a version of E that only considers the jth marked test, which was submitted by the candidate i_j and evaluated with the mark m_j, namely $(i_j, (x_j), m_j) \in \text{Marked}$. Since ProVerif proves that the verifiability-test is complete and sound for one marked test, it follows that for soundness we have

$$\forall 1 \leq j \leq n : MC_1(E_j) \rightarrow^* OK \Rightarrow \text{Correct}(x_j) = m_j$$

and for completeness we have

$$\forall 1 \leq j \leq n : \text{Correct}(x_j) = m_j \Rightarrow MC_1(E_j) \rightarrow^* OK.$$

The verifiability-test $MC_n(E)$ obtains the mark evaluations from channels ch1, ..., chn, and checks if all the tests that are contained in evaluation are marked correctly. The verifiability-test $\forall 1 \leq j \leq n : MC_1(E_j)$ checks if the jth test, whose evaluation is obtained from the channel chj, is marked correctly. Thus, it follows that

```
let testUMC (pkN, bbn, ch1,...,chn) =
 in(bbn, (pseudo_E, he, r, spseE));
 in(ch1, sma1);
 ...
 in(chn, sman);

 let ((ques1, ans1, pseudo_C1), sca1, mark1) =
      checksign(sma1, pseudo_E) in
 ...
 let ((quesn, ansn, pseudo_Cn), scan, markn) =
      checksign(sman, pseudo_E) in
 get correct_ans(ques'1,ans'1,=mark1) in
 ...
 get correct_ans(ques'n,ans'n,=markn) in

 if (pseudo_E, he, r) = checksign(spseE, pkN) && r = E then
  if (ques1=ques'1 && ans'1=ans1)
     &&...&&
     (quesn=ques'n && ans'n=ansn)
  then event OK
  else event KO
 else KO.
```

Figure 5.15: The Marking Correctness universal verifiability-test

$$MC_n(E) \to^* OK$$
$$\Downarrow$$
$$\forall 1 \le j \le n : MC_1(E_j) \to^* OK$$
$$\Downarrow_{(by\ ProVerif)}$$
$$\forall 1 \le j \le n : \texttt{Correct}(x_j) = m_j$$
$$\Downarrow$$
$$\forall(i, (q, a), m) \in \texttt{Marked},\ \texttt{Correct}(x) = m$$

Thus, the verifiability-test $testUMC$ is sound also for the general case.

$$\forall(i, x, m) \in \texttt{Marked},\ \texttt{Correct}(x) = m$$
$$\Downarrow$$
$$\forall 1 \le j \le n : \texttt{Correct}(x_j) = m_j$$
$$\Downarrow_{(by\ ProVerif)}$$
$$\forall 1 \le j \le n : MC_1(E_j) \to^* OK$$
$$\Downarrow$$
$$MC_n(E) \to^* OK$$

Also the verifiability-test $testUMC$ is complete for the general case.

Test Integrity.   The verifiability-test $testUTI$ (Figure 5.16) takes as input from the bulletin board the pseudonyms of the candidates signed by the mixnet and the receipts of submissions plus the mark notifications generated by the exam authority. The auditor can obtain the evaluations generated by the examiner from the mark notifications. The verifiability-test then checks if the submitted tests were marked without any modification. Similarly to Marking Correctness, we assume that one examiner marks all the tests for simplicity.

ProVerif can prove that the verifiability-test is complete and sound when one accepted test and one marked test are considered. To prove the general case that considers an unbounded number of accepted tests, it is necessary to show that

$$testUTI(E) = true \Leftrightarrow \texttt{Accepted} = \{(i, x) : (i, x, m) \in \texttt{Marked}\}$$

holds for an exam execution E that considers any size of the relations $\texttt{Accepted}$ and $\texttt{Marked}$.

It can be assumed that the size of the relation $\texttt{Accepted}$ is equal to the relation $\texttt{Marked}$. In fact, by looking at the bulletin board, the auditor can check that the number of the receipts of submissions coincides with the number of mark notifications.

Let $testUTI_k(\cdot)$ be the Test Integrity verifiability-test applied to an exam execution that has k accepted tests and k marked tests; let $testUTI_k(\cdot) \to^* OK$ denote the verifiability-test that outputs OK (true) after some steps; let E be an exam execution that has n accepted tests and n marked tests; let us assume that the tests are marked in the same order as they were accepted; let E_j be a version of E that only considers the jth accepted test x_j submitted by the candidate i_j, and the jth marked test x'_j associated to the candidate i'_j.

Since ProVerif proves that the verifiability-test is complete and sound for one accepted test and one marked test, it follows that for soundness we have

$$\forall 1 \le j \le n : testUTI_1(E_j) \to^* OK \Rightarrow (i_j, (q_j, a_j)) = (i'_j, (q'_j, a'_j))$$

```
let testUTI(pkN, pkA, bba1,..., bban, bbn, ch1,...,chn)=
 in(bbn, (pseudo_E, he, re, spseE));
 in(ch1,((rcoin1, sca1, pseudo_C1),(rcoinA1, smaA1, pseudo_CA1)));
 ...
 in(chn,((rcoinn, scan, pseudo_Cn),(rcoinAn, smaAn, pseudo_CAn)));
 in(bba1, (receipt1, notif1));
 ...
 in(bban, (receiptn, notifn));

 let (quest1, answ1, pseudo_C'1) = checksign(sca1, pkA) in
 ...
 let (questn, answn, pseudo_C'n) = checksign(scan, pkA) in
 let ((quest'1, answ'1, pseudo_C''1), sca'1, mark1) =
     checksign(smaA1, pseudo_E) in
 ...
 let ((quest'n, answ'n, pseudo_C''n), sca'n, markn) =
     checksign(smaAn, pseudo_E) in

 if (receipt1=int_encrypt((((quest1, answ1, pseudo_C'1), sca1),
                      pseudo_C1, rcoin1) &&
     notif1=int_encrypt(((((quest'1, answ'1, pseudo_C''1), sca'1,
                       mark1), smaA1), pseudo_CA1, rcoinA1) &&
     sca'1=sca1)
     &&...&&
     (receiptn=int_encrypt((((questn, answn, pseudo_C'n), scan),
                      pseudo_Cn, rcoinn)&&
     notifn=int_encrypt(((((quest'n, answ'n, pseudo_C''n), sca'n,
                       markn), smaAn), pseudo_CAn, rcoinAn) &&
     sca'n=scan)
 then
  if (pseudo_C1=pseudo_CA1 && pseudo_CA1=pseudo_C'1 &&
     pseudo_C'1=pseudo_C''1 && quest1=quest'1 && answ1=answ'1)
     &&...&&
     (pseudo_Cn=pseudo_CAn && pseudo_CAn=pseudo_C'n &&
     pseudo_C'n=pseudo_C''n && questn=quest'n && answn=answ'n)
  then event OK
  else KO
 else KO.
```

Figure 5.16: The Test Integrity universal verifiability-test

and for completeness we have

$$\forall 1 \leq j \leq n : (i_j, (q_j, a_j)) = (i'_j, (q'_j, a'_j)) \Rightarrow testUTI_1(E_j) \rightarrow^* OK.$$

The verifiability-test $testUTI_n(E)$ checks if each pair of accepted and marked tests obtained from channels bba1, ..., bban has the same pseudonym, question, and answer. Similarly, the verifiability-test $\forall 1 \leq j \leq n : testUTI_1(E_j)$ checks if the jth accepted and marked tests obtained from the channel bbaj are identical. Thus, it follows that

$$testUTI_n(E) \rightarrow^* OK$$
$$\Downarrow$$
$$\forall 1 \leq j \leq n : testUTI_1(E_j) \rightarrow^* OK$$
$$\Downarrow_{(by\ ProVerif)}$$
$$\forall 1 \leq j \leq n : (i_j, x_j) = (i'_j, x'_j)$$
$$\Downarrow$$
$$\texttt{Accepted} = \{(i, x) : (i, x, m) \in \texttt{Marked}\}$$

Thus, the verifiability-test $testUTI$ is sound also for the general case.

$$\texttt{Accepted} = \{(i, x) : (i, x, m) \in \texttt{Marked}\}$$
$$\Downarrow$$
$$\forall 1 \leq j \leq n : (i_j, x_j) = (i'_j, x'_j)$$
$$\Downarrow$$
$$\forall 1 \leq j \leq n : testUTI_1(E_j) \rightarrow^* OK$$
$$\Downarrow$$
$$testUTI_n(E) \rightarrow^* OK$$

Also the verifiability-test $testUTI$ is complete for the general case.

Test Markedness. Since Remark! is test integrity universally verifiable, it is also test markedness universally verifiable. The proof strategy is the same outlined above for Test Integrity. However, it is not necessary to assume that the size of the relation Accepted is equal to the relation Marked, since Test Markedness does not require strict equality of the two multisets.

Mark Integrity. The verifiability-test $testUMI$, which is in Figure 5.17, is fed with mark notifications posted on the bulletin board by the exam authority. The auditor obtains the evaluations generated by the examiner from the mark notifications, and checks if the marks that the exam authority assigned to the candidates coincide with the marks that the examiner assigned to the candidates' tests. Also for this requirement we assume one examiner who marks all the tests.

In the case that the relations Assigned and Marked contain each one entry, ProVerif proves that the verifiability-test Mark Integrity is complete and sound. The general case, which considers an unbounded number of entries, consists on proving that

$$testUMI(E) = true \Leftrightarrow \texttt{Assigned} = \{(i, m) : (i, x, m) \in \texttt{Marked}\}$$

holds for an exam execution E that considers any size of the relations Assigned and Marked.

```
let testUMI (bbn, bba1,...,bban) =
 in(bbn, (pseudo_E, he, re, spseE));
 in(bba1, (notif1,rcoin1, sma1));
 ...
 in(bban, (notifn,rcoinn, sman));

 let ((quest1, answ1, pseudo_C1), sca'1, mark1) =
     checksign(sma1, pseudo_E) in
 ...
 let ((questn, answn, pseudo_Cn), sca'n, markn) =
     checksign(sman, pseudo_E) in

 if notif1=int_encrypt(((((quest1, answ1, pseudo_C1),sca'1, mark1),
                     sma1), pseudo_C1, rcoin1)
    &&...&&
    notifn=int_encrypt(((((questn, answn, pseudo_Cn),sca'n, markn),
                     sman), pseudo_Cn, rcoinn)
 then event OK
 else event KO.
```

Figure 5.17: The Mark Integrity universal verifiability-test

Similarly to Test Integrity, it can be assumed that the size of the relation **Assigned** is equal to the relation **Marked**, as the auditor can check such equality by looking at the bulletin board.

Let $testUMI_k(\cdot)$ be the Mark Integrity verifiability-test applied to an exam execution that has k marks assigned to the candidates and k marks associated to the tests; let $testUMI_k(\cdot) \to^* OK$ denote the verifiability-test that outputs OK (true) after some steps; let E be an exam execution that has n marks assigned to the candidates and n marks associated to the candidates' tests; let us assume that the tests are assigned to the candidates in the same order as they were marked; let E_j be a version of E that only considers the jth mark m_j assigned to the candidate i_j, and the jth mark m'_j associated to the test of candidate j'_j.

Since ProVerif proves that the verifiability-test is complete and sound for one entry, it follows that for soundness we have

$$\forall 1 \leq j \leq n : testUMI_1(E_j) \to^* OK \Rightarrow (i_j, m_j) = (i'_j, m'_j)$$

and for completeness we have

$$\forall 1 \leq j \leq n : (i_j, m_j) = (i'_j, m'_j) \Rightarrow testUMI_1(E_j) \to^* OK.$$

The verifiability-test $testUMI_n(E)$ receives from the channels bba1, ..., bban the notifications of the exam authority, and checks if the pseudonyms and marks obtained from the notifications coincide with the ones obtained from the evaluations of the examiner. Similarly, the verifiability-test $\forall 1 \leq j \leq n : testUMI_1(E_j)$ checks if the jth pseudonym and mark obtained from the evaluation and notification on channel bbaj are identical. Thus, it follows that

Requirement	Soundness	Completeness
Registration	✓	✓(all)
Marking Correctness	✓ (EA)	✓(all)
Test Integrity	✓	✓(all)
Test Markedness	✓	✓(all)
Mark Integrity	✓	✓(all)

Table 5.4: Summary of the analysis of Remark! for U.V. requirements

$$testUMI_n(E) \to^* OK$$
$$\Downarrow$$
$$\forall 1 \le j \le n : testUMI_1(E_j) \to^* OK$$
$$\Downarrow_{(by\ ProVerif)}$$
$$\forall 1 \le j \le n : (i_j, m_j) = (i'_j, m'_j)$$
$$\Downarrow$$
$$\{(i, m) : (i, x, m) \in \texttt{Marked}\} = \texttt{Assigned}$$

Thus, the verifiability-test *testUMI* is sound also for the general case.

$$\{(i, m) : (i, x, m) \in \texttt{Marked}\} = \texttt{Assigned}$$
$$\Downarrow$$
$$\forall 1 \le j \le n : (i_j, m_j) = (i'_j, m'_j)$$
$$\Downarrow_{(by\ ProVerif)}$$
$$\forall 1 \le j \le n : testUMI_1(E_j) \to^* OK$$
$$\Downarrow$$
$$testUMI_n(E) \to^* OK$$

Thus, the verifiability-test *testUMI* is complete also for the general case.

Table 5.4 summarises the results of the universal verifiability analysis of Remark! and reports the roles required to be honest.

5.5   Conclusion

This chapter presents Remark!, a protocol for Internet-based exams that guarantees authentication, privacy, and verifiability with minimal trust assumptions. Remark! meets its requirements in most of the cases by assuming only one honest server among the servers that compose the exponentiation mixnet. According to each requirement, Remark! can resist against the collusion of candidate and exam authority (e.g., Anonymous Examiner), exam authority and examiner (e.g., Anonymous Marking), or candidate and examiner (e.g., Question Indistinguishability) without the presence of a trusted third party.

A formal analysis in ProVerif confirms that Remark! ensures all the authentication and privacy requirements proposed in Chapter 3. Notably, thanks to this formal analysis, we found and solved an issue with an earlier version of the protocol.

Remark! proves to be fully verifiable, according to the individual and universal verifiability definitions proposed in Chapter 3. ProVerif automatically validates all the individual verifiability requirements. All the requirements but Question Validity and Marking Correctness can be proved in the presence of an honest mixnet and corrupted candidates, examiners, and exam authority. Question Validity and Marking Correctness still require an honest exam authority. Concerning the universal verifiability requirements, ProVerif cannot deal with the general cases. Thus, we completed the analysis with manual proofs. It turns out that Remark! ensures all the requirements but Marking Correctness assuming corrupted candidates, examiners, and exam authority. Also, in this case, Marking Correctness can be proved, assuming an honest exam authority. However, it is needed that the exam authority provides the auditor with some additional data at the conclusion of the exam, since all the messages posted on the bulletin board are encrypted.

Chapter 6

The WATA Family

In this chapter, we focus on a family of computer-assisted exam protocols called *WATA*, which stands for Written Authenticated Though Anonymous exams. A common characteristic of all WATA protocols is the traditional testing procedure, which is face-to-face. The difference among the WATA protocols is that each version provides a different level of computer assistance. Additionally, each protocol of the family has some slightly different functional requirement and threat model with respect to the others. One protocol considers local tasks, such as notification of marks, and no TTP. Some others consider remote tasks, such as remote registration, but assume TTP. Another achieves remote tasks without TTP. In some way, Remark! already makes remote registration and remote notification with minimal reliance on trusted parties. As Remark! belongs to the class of Internet-based exams, it mandates candidate and exam authority to use computers at testing to sign and encrypt the tests. Therefore, testing cannot take place by pen and paper. Moreover, Remark! assumes at least one honest mix server. As we shall see later, there exists a version of WATA that ensures the same authentication and privacy requirements of Remark! without the need to rely on mixnet or TTP.

The various versions of WATA progressively introduce more computer assistance in their design still keeping traditional testing. The design of WATA I, II, and III has a high reliance on trusted parties. The design of WATA IV sees a lightweight participation of a TTP, and also opens up for computer-based exams. Moreover, it ensures more security requirements despite a stronger threat model. WATA IV is further reconceived to completely remove the TTP by combining oblivious transfer and visual cryptography to allow candidate and examiner to jointly generate a pseudonym that anonymises the candidate's test. This pseudonym is revealed only to the candidate at the beginning of the face-to-face testing. This latter protocol proves to be secure by a formal analysis in ProVerif, which demonstrates that the protocol meets all the stated security requirements.

This chapter provides descriptions of all the WATA protocols available in the literature. It allows us to appreciate the different trade-offs between functional and security requirements in each of the WATA version.

© Springer International Publishing AG 2018
R. Giustolisi, *Modelling and Verification of Secure Exams*, Information Security
and Cryptography, https://doi.org/10.1007/978-3-319-67107-9_6

Notification Request Authentication

The WATA exam was originally conceived for university exams, and in some universities nowadays candidates can take the exam up to a fixed number of times. However, if the candidate withdraws, it is not counted towards the number of attempts. Other universities have a policy that does not allow the candidate to resit a failed exam the next session, unless the candidate withdraws from the exam before notification. Thus, WATA exams consider the additional requirement of *Notification Request Authentication*. It says that a mark should be associated with the candidate only if she requests to learn her mark.

To formalise this requirement in the applied π-calculus, we need to define two new events that extend the list proposed in Chapter 3.

- requested$\langle id\_c, id\_test \rangle$ means that the candidate id_c accepts to learn the mark associated to the test id_test. The event is inserted into the process of the candidate at the location where the request is sent to the notifier.

- stored$\langle id\_c, mark \rangle$ means that the authority officially considers the candidate id_c associated with $mark$. The event is inserted into the process of the authority at the location where it registers the mark to the candidate.

The requirement can be specified as follows:

Definition 43 (Notification Request Authentication) *An exam protocol ensures* Notification Request Authentication *if for every exam process EP*

$$\text{stored}\langle id\_c, mark \rangle \;\rightsquigarrow\; \text{inj} \, \text{requested}\langle id\_c, id\_test \rangle$$

on every execution trace.

We use the specification above to formally analyse the protocol described in Section 6.5.

Outline of the chapter.   Section 6 discusses existing schemes for computer-assisted and computer-based exams. Section 6.2 describes WATA I & II protocols and their informal analyses. Section 6.3 details WATA III. Section 6.4 introduces WATA IV according to the four phases of an exam and points up the novel security aspects respect to the previous WATA schemes. Section 6.5 redesigns parts of WATA IV to remove the TTP. It also introduces the formalisation of dispute resolution, and provides the formal analysis of the protocol in ProVerif. Section 6.6 discusses future work and ends the chapter.

6.1   Computer-Assisted and Computer-Based Exams

Nowadays, most of the exams employed in public competitions are computer-assisted or even computer-based. ETS and Pearson Vue develop various Computer-assisted exams for skill and professional certifications [ETS15, Pea15]. The European Union adopts computer-based exams for the selection of EU personnel [Off13]. The specification of such exams is not publicly available, and their security fully relies on the developers, who have the prominent role of TTP during the exam execution. This choice has not prevented frauds on the administered exams [Wat14].

Different exam protocols have been proposed to ensure anonymous marking. INFOSAFE [INF15] is an anonymous marking system for computer-assisted exam with traditional testing, and is adopted in university exams. Candidates write down their personal details on top of a tamper-evident paper, and hide them with a flap which is bent and glued over. After marking, the personal details are disclosed by tearing off the flap. Systems following a "double envelope" strategy, often used in public tenders, make use of two envelops to separate the identification details from the offers. The personal details are assumed to be read after marking. Many European universities, such as Dublin City University and University of Sheffield, use their own anonymous marking systems [Uni15, oS15]. So do top USA academies, such as Stanford and Harvard Law School [Sch15, Lev04]. The latter relies on the Blind Grading Number system which assigns candidates with numerical pseudonyms until the marking period ends. Nemo Scan [Neo15] uses a patented anonymity paper cover [Mou09] consisting of two parts: one with the covered candidate details, the other with a section where to type the marks. At notification, a scanner with a proprietary software reads the paper with the candidate details and assigns her the mark.

All the systems outlined above assume a trusted authority to ensure Anonymous Marking. Moreover, it is not clear how such systems scale up to other security requirements. In this chapter, we discuss how to progressively remove trusted authorities from the design of the protocols, and consider the exam authority corrupted to various extents.

6.2 WATA I & II

The WATA exams were originally developed at the University of Catania and have two main goals historically. The first goal is to mechanise the double envelope technique in a software. The second goal is to ensure authentication and anonymity despite a corrupted examiner.

The first two versions of the system are conceptually identical and only differ in the implementations: WATA I was written in Visual Basic and was only available for Microsoft Windows; WATA II [BCR10] was implemented in Java, hence more efficient and portable. In this chapter, we only focus on the second version.

WATA II considers the roles of examiner, invigilator, and candidate. The examiner, in addition to the usual tasks assigned to its role, runs tasks normally ascribed to other authorities, such as the question committee, the recorder and the notifier. The invigilator distributes the tests to the candidates, and collects them at the end of testing. Every phase of the exam is executed locally, and testing takes place traditionally by pen and paper.

The examiner maintains data in three tables: the history table DB_h records the performances of the candidate over the past exam; the mark table DB_m stores the mark assigned to each test; The question table DB_q stores the questions.

In the following, we describe the protocol and refer to the message sequence chart depicted in Figure 6.1.

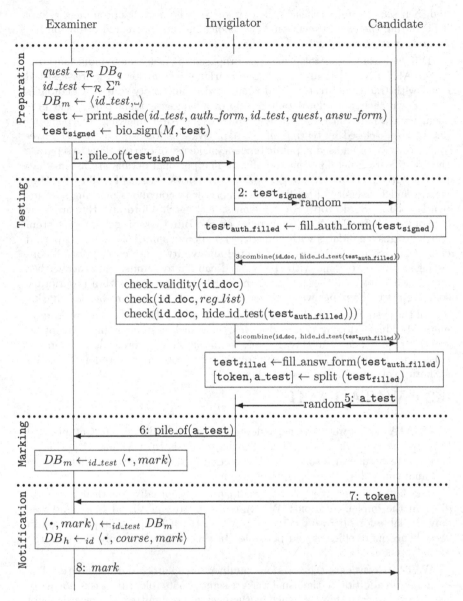

Figure 6.1: The WATA II exam protocol

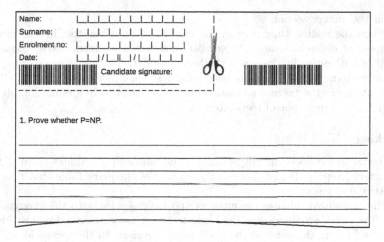

Figure 6.2: Fragment of a test in WATA II

Preparation

The examiner randomly extracts a list of questions *quest* from the question table, and generates a random test identifier *id_test* of predetermined size n using the alphabet Σ. The test identifier is stored in the mark table next to an empty mark. The examiner then prints out the **test**, which contains the following information: the test identifier *id_test*, an authentication form *auth_form*, another occurrence of the test identifier, the questions, and a form for the answers *answ_form*. To facilitate the mechanical reading, both occurrences of the test identifier are encoded as a barcode. The test has a precise layout, notably with test identifier and authentication form framed at the top-left corner of the sheet through a dotted line; this can be seen in Figure 6.2. The examiner signs inside this frame across test identifier and authentication form and possibly reinforces the signature with the stamp of the exam organisation. It is assumed that this association is tamper-proof. This produces **test**$_{signed}$, which the examiner hands to the invigilator (step 1). This phase is repeated as many times as the number of registered candidates, so that the invigilator gets a pile of tests pre-signed by the examiner.

Testing

The invigilator leaves the pile of tests on a desk at the exam venue. Then, the candidate picks a test randomly (step 2), and is assigned a seat. At her seat, the candidate fills out the authentication form with her personal details, and temporarily hides the test identifier prior to hand the test combined with her identity document to the invigilator for authentication (step 3). The hiding could be achieved, for example, by folding the top corners in. In so doing, the invigilator cannot learn the test identifier while authenticating the candidate. The invigilator checks whether the identity document is the candidate's valid one, whether the candidate identity matches an entry in the list of registered candidates and the details written on the authentication form. If so, the invigilator hands identity document and test back to the candidate (step 4), who can fill out the answer section.

When the testing time is over, the candidate tears the test in two pieces of papers of different sizes. The smaller one, which we term *token*, contains the filled authentication form and the test identifier. The larger piece of paper, which we term *a_test*, contains questions, test identifier, and answers. The candidate keeps the *token*, and leaves the anonymous test in a random position through the current pile of tests (step 5).

Marking

The invigilator collects the pile of anonymous tests and distributes them to the examiners (step 6). It also removes the records of the mark table that refer to undistributed tests.

The examiner evaluates the answers and assigns a mark to the anonymous test. The examiner then scans the barcode to get the corresponding test identifier, and enters the mark in the mark table, precisely in the record identified by the test identifier.

Notification

The candidate who wants to know her mark brings her token at the venue announced to host the notification. There the candidate hands the token to the examiner (step 7), who checks signature and personal details, and scans the barcode to get the corresponding test identifier. The examiner finds the record identified by the test identifier on the mark table, and obtains the corresponding mark. Finally, the examiner stores the mark into the history table, and notifies the mark to the candidate (step 8).

Discussion

Except for the preparation of the tests, the presence of computers in WATA II is minimal. Most of the tasks are run by humans, and the security of the protocol mostly relies on the physical properties of paper.

We consider the requirements proposed in Chapter 3. It can be observed that WATA II trivially ensures Test Authenticity but not Anonymous Examiner because the protocol considers only one examiner. Candidate Authorisation is met because the invigilator authorises the candidate to take the exam only if the personal details reported on the identity document match an entry in the list of eligible candidates. Also Answer Authenticity is met because the invigilator verifies that the candidate wrote the personal details on the authentication form. Moreover, the examiner's signature on the tests ensures their authenticity. It follows that WATA II also ensures Test Origin Authentication. Mark Authenticity is met because the examiner inserts the mark into the mark table, exactly in the record identified by the random test identifier reported into the test. At notification, the examiner notifies the candidate with this mark, which is also stored in the history table. However, a malicious examiner may tell a different mark after the candidate hands him the token. The novel requirement of Notification Request Authentication is met because only the candidate holds the token. A malicious examiner cannot generate a forged token because it would need to be signed by the candidate. In fact, the candidate is the sole entity who can establish the link between her identity and her test.

Concerning privacy requirements, WATA II guarantees Question Indistinguishability provided that the candidate does not collude either with the examiner or the invigilator. In fact, the examiner hands the tests to the invigilator prior testing. However, if the questions that appear into a test are randomly chosen, it becomes harder for a candidate to learn which questions she will be assigned. Anonymous Marking is met because only the candidate knows the test identifier associated to her. Moreover, the candidate submits the test in a random position of the pile of anonymous tests. WATA II ensures Mark Privacy because the notification is face-to-face. The examiner notifies the mark to the corresponding candidate after a successful authentication, and only if she hands a valid token. Since Mark Privacy is met, it follows that also Mark Anonymity is met.

Although WATA II ensures authentication and privacy without TTP, it has the major limitation that notification requires candidates to meet in person the examiner.

6.3   WATA III

WATA III [BCCKR11] redesigns completely the protocol to offer a major level of computer assistance, remote management and remote notification — features not available in the previous versions. The protocol considers the participation of the *WATA Server* in addition to candidate, examiner, and invigilator roles. The WATA Server runs most of the tasks of preparation and notification, while the tasks of the examiner are now limited to the marking phase.

The WATA Server maintains data in four tables. The history, mark, and question tables have the same functionalities of the previous protocol. WATA III introduces the *sharec* table DB_c that stores the partial information about the test identifier, which now is called *pseudonym*.

The pseudonym is associated also to the candidate rather than only to the test. The idea is to split the pseudonym in two shares, print them on the test, and give one to the candidate and the other to the examiner. The latter can associate a test to its author only if the candidate reveals its share.

WATA III assumes that a list of registered candidates for the exam is available to the invigilator, and secure TLS communications between the WATA Server and the other principals. The WATA Server authenticates invigilator and candidate via login and password. Every communication between invigilator and candidate is face-to-face, while communications to the WATA Server are always remote. Remote communications are highlighted with dashed lines in the message sequence chart in Figure 6.3.

Remark.   The original specification of WATA III [BCCKR11] is affected by a security issue. In a nutshell, the specification allowed a corrupted candidate to be assigned with the mark of the test submitted by another candidate, hence violating Mark Authenticity. The corrupted candidate could generate a fake pseudonym such that at notification she could convince the examiner that the pseudonym should associated with her identity. This was possible because the original specification contemplates a weak generation of the pseudonym that reveals key information. This issue can be fixed by hiding such information via hashing. In the remainder, we only describe the fixed version.

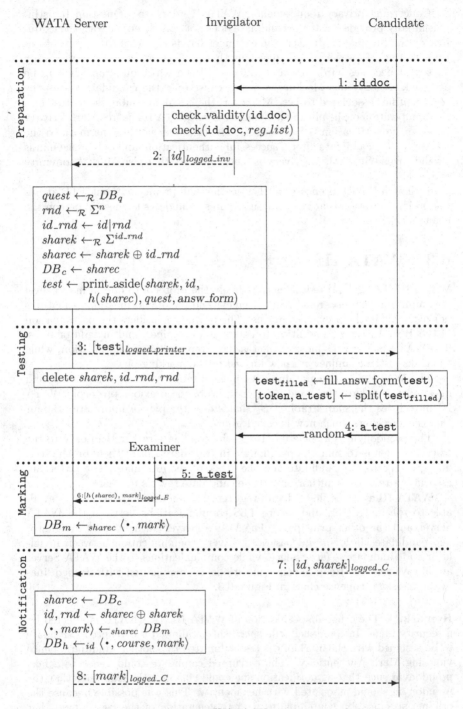

Figure 6.3: The WATA III exam protocol

Preparation

At exam venue, the candidate approaches the invigilator's desk and hands her identity document id_doc (step 1). The invigilator checks whether the personal details of the candidate id appears in the registered candidate list, and if so, logs in the WATA Server and sends id via secure channel (step 2). The WATA Server randomly extracts the questions from the question table. Then, it generates a random value $sharek$, whose length matches the id augmented with some randomness id_rnd. Thus, it generates ($sharec$) that is the result of the one-time pad of $sharek$ with id_rnd. The WATA Server stores $sharec$ in the database and finally generates the layout of the test. The $sharek$ is placed on the top left of the printout, while the hashed version of $sharec$ is placed on the top right of the printout, close to the answer section $answ\_form$. Both $sharek$ and hashed $sharec$ are represented in the form of barcode. The test thus consists of two parts: the $token$, which contains $sharek$ and the candidate's personal details id; the anonymous test a_test, which contains the hash of $sharec$, questions, and answer section.

Testing

The WATA Server sends the test via a secure channel to a printer, which is available at the exam venue. The candidate approaches the printer and takes its test (step 3). Then, the WATA Server deletes all the data it used but the one stored in the tables, namely it removes $sharek$, id_rnd, and the randomness.

At her seat, the candidate fills out the answer section with the answers. When the time is over, the candidate splits the test, and takes the token at home while inserts the anonymous test a_test into a random position of the pile of anonymous tests (step 4).

Marking

The invigilator collects the pile of anonymous tests and hands them to the examiner (step 5), who evaluates the answers and assigns a mark to each anonymous test. For each test, the examiner scans the barcode and gets the corresponding hash of $sharec$. The examiner then logs into WATA Server and uploads the pair of hashed $sharec$ and mark via a secure channel (step 6). The WATA Server can find the corresponding $sharec$ by hashing each entry of DB_c. In so doing, it can store the mark in the entry identified by $sharec$ in the mark table.

Notification

The candidate who wants to know her mark scans the barcode printed in the token and gets $sharek$, which she sends to the WATA Server via a secure channel, after she logged in (step 7). The WATA Server XOR-es $sharek$ with each $sharec$ stored in the database until it decrypts a valid id concatenated with some randomness. It then retrieves the record identified by the $sharec$ from the mark table, and obtains the corresponding mark. Finally, the WATA Server stores the mark into the history table, and notifies it to the candidate (step 8).

Discussion

It is clear that WATA III cannot be deemed secure assuming a corrupted WATA Server. This role is ubiquitous in the design and is in charge of the critical steps. Therefore, the WATA Server should be considered as an honest-but-curious role, which follows the protocol honestly but tries to learn as much as possible.

A critical part of the protocol is the deletion of data performed by the WATA Server. Although this practice is found in other protocols [EKOT14], it may be impractical to force a party to delete data. However, it can be still possible to verify that the party actually deletes the data [HCZ15].

Concerning the authentication requirements, WATA III ensures Candidate Authorisation since the invigilator authorises the candidate to take the exam only if the candidate's personal details reported on the valid identity document match an entry in the list of eligible candidates. The invigilator has to ensure that the correct candidate takes the test generated for her from the printer. This avoids that corrupted candidates swap their tests before sitting for the exam. In fact, the protocol does not require that the candidate writes her personal details down into the test as provided for the previous version. Thus, the invigilator does not need to check the test once the candidate sits for the exam. Answer Authenticity is met because candidates are invigilated. If a corrupted candidate introduces an illegal test, she will not be able to receive a mark because the examiner would upload a forged hash of *sharec* that the WATA Server could not retrieve in the database. It follows that WATA III ensures Test Origin Authentication. Similarly to WATA II, Test Authenticity is met but not Anonymous Examiner since the protocol considers only one examiner. Mark Authenticity is met because both candidate and examiner know only the hash of *sharec* until notification. WATA III ensures Notification request authentication because only the candidate knows the *sharek* after testing.

Concerning privacy requirements, Question Indistinguishability is met because the WATA Server generates the test with the questions. Each test is printed at testing and taken by the candidate directly, so the invigilator learns the question only when testing concludes. Although the WATA Server deletes some data at testing, we observe that it can violate Anonymous Marking. At preparation, a corrupted WATA Server can associate the candidate *id* with the corresponding *sharec*. At testing, the WATA Server receives from the examiner the mark associated with the hash of the *sharec*. Therefore, the WATA Server can learn the author of a test without the knowledge of *sharek*. Note that this attack is possible even considering an honest-but-curious threat model because it does not require that the WATA Server deviates from the protocol, but resorts solely on the knowledge of the WATA Server. Finally, Mark Privacy is met because the WATA Server notifies the mark to the candidate only, after receiving a correct *sharek*. It follows that WATA III ensures Mark Anonymity as well.

WATA III allows for remote notification but assigns most of its critical tasks to a TTP. It turns out that considering an honest-but-curious WATA Server, WATA III fails to ensure Anonymous Marking.

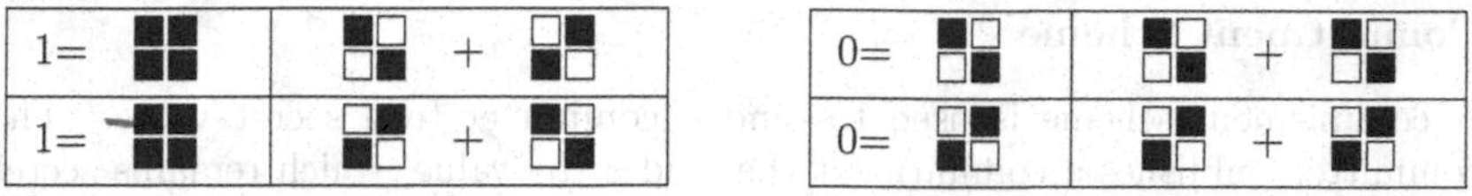

Figure 6.4: Representation of bits 0 and 1 using visual cryptography

6.4 WATA IV

WATA IV aims to minimise the involvement of the TTP that the new design of WATA III introduces in all the phases of the exam. Specifically, WATA IV removes the ubiquitous WATA Server role and introduces the *anonymiser*, whose participation is confined to preparation only. Similar to the WATA Server, the anonymiser is honest-but-curious but its duties are drastically reduced. In WATA IV most of the critical tasks are run by a possibly corrupted examiner. Moreover, WATA IV opens for remote preparation and requires no printers at testing. We anticipate that WATA IV meets the same security requirements as WATA III does, though augmented with Anonymous Marking and the two individual verifiability requirements of Mark Integrity and Mark Notification Integrity.

The main novelty of the design of WATA IV is the use of visual cryptography. The idea consists of encoding the pseudonym into two visual cryptographic shares: one share is given to the candidate, and the other is given to the examiner. Neither the candidate nor the examiner knows the pseudonym until they meet at testing, when the candidate learns the pseudonym by overlapping the examiner's share with hers.

Thanks to visual cryptography, the candidate can do a cryptographic operation at testing without the assistance of any computer device. In the following, we briefly discuss visual cryptography and commitment scheme, namely the cryptographic primitives used in WATA IV.

Visual Cryptography

It is a secret sharing scheme, devised by Naor and Shamir [NS95], that allows a visual decryption of a ciphertext. A secret image is "encrypted" by splitting it into a number of image *shares*. The basic version of the scheme is the 2-out-of-2 secret sharing system, in which a secret image is split into two shares $share_A$ and $share_B$. The shares are printed on transparency sheets, which reveal the secret image when the shares are overlapped. This scheme is information-theoretic secure, namely each share leaks no information about the secret image. In fact, it emulates the XOR operation though the visual decryption is actually equivalent to the OR operation. The scheme is information-theoretic secure because either a black or a white pixel, mapped respectively to 0 and 1, can originate by any of the sub-pixels shown in Figure 6.4.

Many schemes for visual cryptography have been proposed over the years. Although we consider the Naor and Shamir scheme for WATA IV, we conjecture that other visual scheme can be used as well, but with different security guarantees.

Commitment Scheme

A commitment scheme is used to bind a committer to a secret value. The committer publishes a commitment that hides the value, which remains secret until he reveals it. Should the committer reveal a different value, this would be noticed because it cannot be mapped to the published commitment. WATA IV uses the Pedersen commitment scheme [Ped92], which guarantees unconditional hiding, namely the value remains secret despite a computational unbounded attacker. The scheme consists of the algorithms of *commitment*, in which the value is chosen, hidden, and bound to the committer, and of *disclosure*, in which the value is publicly revealed. The commitment algorithm takes in two given public generators $g, h \in \mathbb{G}_q$, the secret value v, and a random value $r \in_{\mathcal{R}} \mathbb{Z}_q^*$. The algorithm outputs the commitment $g^v h^r$ denoted with $C_r(v)$. The disclosure algorithm takes in the commitment $C_r(v)$, the values v and r, and outputs `true` if the commitment is correct or `false` otherwise.

WATA IV adopts the Pedersen commitment scheme at notification. The examiner generates a commitment of the mark of the candidate. Once the candidate reveals her identity to know the mark, she can verify the examiner notifies her the committed mark. This deters the examiner to notify the candidate with a mark that is different than the one assigned to candidate's test.

Description

WATA IV relies on an append-only bulletin board in which the examiner publishes the pseudonyms and the commitment of the marks. Each session is identified with a unique exam code *ex*. In the following we describe the protocol and refer to the message sequence chart depicted in Figure 6.5.

Preparation

The examiner checks the candidate eligible for the exam *ex* and, if so, enters the candidate details *id* in the dedicated list *reg_list*. After that, the examiner sends the candidate's details and the exam code to the anonymiser via a secure channel (step 1).

The anonymiser generates the pseudonym *pid* that consists of a visual representation of a random alphanumeric string, and a random visual cryptographic image, *share*$_A$. Then, the anonymiser generates the second visual cryptographic image, *share*$_B$, such that overlapping *share*$_A$ and *share*$_B$ results in the image representing of the pseudonym. Let *data*$_A$ denote the triplet of *id*, *ex* and *share*$_A$. The anonymiser signs *data*$_A$, and generates the corresponding signature as follows. First, the plaintexts *data*$_A$ and *data*$_B$ are encoded in *Base64* and signed with the signing key of the anonymiser SSK_{An}. Then, the signatures are encoded in *Base64* again, and included in two QR codes with the corresponding encoded plaintext. To facilitate the printing, the anonymiser includes such information in the digital versions of an A4 paper sheet, respectively *transp* and *paper*, which layout is outlined in Figure 6.6. The signatures printed on the bottom of the sheets self contain the data reported on each sheet plus the corresponding signature. The anonymiser emails *transp* to the examiner (step 2) and *paper* to the candidate (step 3). We assume that the attacker is out of control of the email infrastructure, hence he cannot learn the contents. However

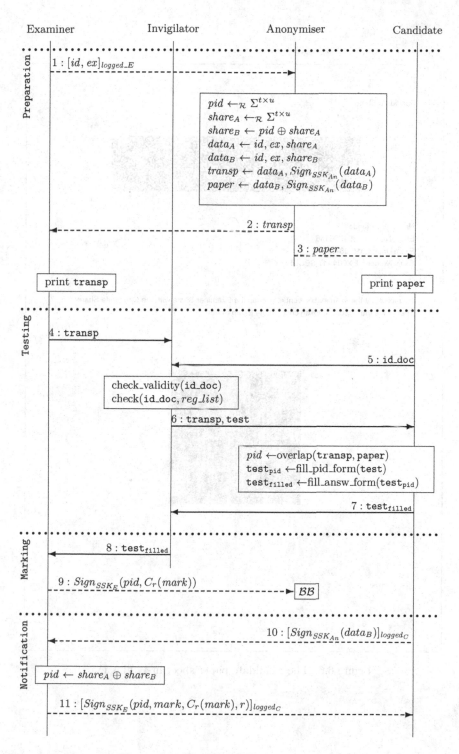

Figure 6.5: The WATA IV exam protocol

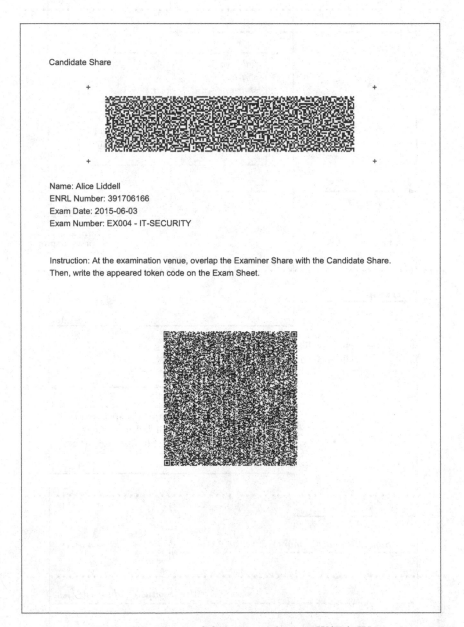

Candidate Share

Name: Alice Liddell
ENRL Number: 391706166
Exam Date: 2015-06-03
Exam Number: EX004 - IT-SECURITY

Instruction: At the examination venue, overlap the Examiner Share with the Candidate Share.
Then, write the appeared token code on the Exam Sheet.

Figure 6.6: The candidate paper sheet in WATA IV

secure emailing techniques, such as S/MIME [RT10] or MIME over OpenPGP [EDTLR01], can be used to ensure confidentiality of the content of the emails.

For each candidate, the examiner stores the signed *data$_A$* into the database, and prints each `transp` on a transparency sheet. Similarly, each candidate prints her `paper` on a common A4 paper sheet.

Testing

The examiner hands the transparency sheet to the invigilator (step 4). The candidate takes a seat at exam venue, and hands a valid identity document `id_doc` to the invigilator for authentication (step 5). The invigilator checks that the candidate is in the list of those registered for the exam. Then, the invigilator finds the transparency sheet `transp` that reports the candidate's details, and hands it to her along with a `test` (step 6). If some registered candidates fail to show up, the invigilator puts the corresponding transparency sheets and the excess tests aside.

Once the invigilator delivers the transparency sheets to all candidates, the candidate can overlap her paper sheet with the corresponding transparency sheet and can read the pseudonym. The candidate writes down the pseudonym into the test and begins to answer the questions. When the testing time is over, the candidate submits her test (step 7), and takes the paper and transparency sheets back with her. The candidate can place her test anywhere in the pile of already submitted tests. The invigilator collects the pile of tests when all candidates have submitted their tests.

Marking

The invigilator hands all the tests (step 8) and the remaining transparency sheets to the examiner. The examiner evaluates the test, generates a commitment of the *mark*, signs the pair of pseudonym and mark (*pid, mark*) and publishes the signature on the public append-only bulletin board (step 9). This allows the candidate to verify whether her test has been marked though ignoring the mark.

Notification

The examiner runs notification for a fixed time frame. The candidate who wants to know her mark sends the signed *data$_B$* to the examiner via a secure channel (step 10). The examiner verifies the signature, and overlaps *share$_B$* with its *share$_A$* to get the pseudonym *pid*. Notably, this procedure can be implemented, hence requires no human involvement. The examiner thus retrieves the mark associated with the pseudonym, and finally sends to the candidate the signature of pseudonym, mark, commitment, and commitment random value (step 11).

Discussion

WATA IV ensures all the security requirements as WATA III and a few more. Concerning authentication, Test Authenticity is trivially met while Anonymous Examiner is not because the protocol assumes only one examiner. Candidate Authorisation is met because the invigilator checks that the candidate is in the list of those registered for the exam. Answer Authenticity is met because the invigilator gives to the candidate the transparency sheet that has her details. If a corrupted candidate prints a different visual crypto image on her paper sheet, she cannot read any intelligible pseudonym by overlapping the paper sheet with the transparency sheet. The same applies if any two corrupted candidates swap their paper sheets before testing. As we shall see later, a dispute resolution procedure guarantees that a corrupted candidate cannot even claim that no pseudonym appears because the examiner misprinted the transparency sheet. Still, a corrupted candidate could write a random pseudonym into the test, but at notification the candidate would not be able to send a valid $data_B$. Since WATA IV ensures Candidate Authorisation and Answer Authenticity, it also ensures Test Origin Authentication. Mark Authenticity is met because the examiner posts on the bulletin board the signature of the pseudonym associated with a commitment of the mark. Notification request authentication is also met because only the candidate holds her $share_B$.

Concerning privacy, Question Indistinguishability is met by the assumptions on the origin of tests, in which the examiner generates the tests. WATA IV guarantees Anonymous Marking because the examiner cannot associate a test with a candidate until notification. Anonymous Marking can last forever, even if examiner and the invigilator collude, provided that the candidate chooses not to get her mark. Mark Privacy is met because the examiner notifies the mark to the candidate only if the latter sends a valid $share_B$. Thus each candidate can get only their corresponding mark. Notably, the anonymiser cannot associate a candidate with a mark, because the examiner only publishes the commitment of the mark on the bulletin board. It follows that also Mark Anonymity is met.

Concerning the individual verifiability requirements, Mark Integrity is met because the candidates can verify that the examiner registered the same mark whose commitment was published on the bulletin board. Similarly, Mark Notification Integrity is met because the candidate can verify that the mark notified by the examiner is the same committed on the bulletin board.

Dispute Resolution

An interesting feature of WATA IV is the support for dispute resolution during testing. The combination of signatures and visual cryptography guarantees an easy procedure to find the culprit if the candidate and/or the examiner misbehave. Therefore, Dispute Resolution qualifies as an accountability requirement as it enables a judge to blame the principal who misbehave in the execution of the protocol.

In WATA IV the judge is the invigilator, and the dispute originates if no intelligible pseudonym can be read when the candidate overlaps the paper sheet with the transparency sheet. Should such a dispute arise, the invigilator could then quickly resolve it as follows. First, he scans the QR code printed on the candidate's paper sheet and checks the correctness of the signature. Then, he checks if the candidate's details revealed by the signature match the ones written on the candidate's paper sheet. If so, the invigilator overlaps the visual crypto image revealed by the signature with the transparency sheet provided by the examiner. If this reveals no intelligible pseudonym then the examiner misprinted the corresponding transparency sheet. Otherwise the candidate misprinted hers. The outcome of the dispute can be double checked by repeating the procedure with the QR code printed on the transparency sheet of the examiner.

Comparison with WATA III

WATA IV brings along significant improvements compared to WATA III. In particular:

- WATA IV meets the same security requirements of WATA III augmented with Anonymous Marking and the two individual verifiability requirements of Mark Integrity and Mark Notification Integrity.

- WATA IV meets the security requirements despite a more realistic threat model as it drastically limits the tasks assigned to honest-but-curious roles.

- WATA IV can support both computer-based and computer-assisted exams, while WATA III supports only computer-assisted exams with traditional testing. This is possible because test and pseudonym are generated independently in WATA IV. At testing, the candidate chooses one of the computer devices provided at exam venue, and enters the pseudonym retrieved from the paper sheets. Of course, the use of computers at testing raises similar security of Internet-based exam, as discussed in Chapter 5 for Remark!.

- In WATA IV the candidate receives part of the pseudonym by mail rather than at the exam venue.

- In WATA IV the examiner cannot register a different mark to the candidate after he learns the corresponding test, because he commits the mark at marking.

- In WATA IV any dispute between the candidate and the examiner can be solved with no efforts at testing: if an intelligible pseudonym appears, the candidate received the correct transparency sheet. If not, the signatures on the sheets reveal who misbehaved.

In the next section we discuss an enhancement that removes the need for the honest-but-curios anonymiser in the design of the protocol. Moreover, the results of the informal security analysis outlined above are validated via the automated verification of the enhanced protocol in ProVerif.

6.5   WATA Without TTP

The major limitation of WATA IV is that it requires an honest-but-curious anonymiser. Although its lightweight participation, relying on a trusted third party in the design of a security protocol introduces obvious risks. The risks can be mitigated by distributing the trust across several parties, as seen for Remark! in Chapter 5, but it still requires at least one party (i.e., a mix server) to be trustworthy. In the domain of exams this is critical because parties typically have conflicting interests, and it may be hard to find an entity who can play the role of a TTP.

In this section, we discuss an enhancement to WATA IV that guarantees several security properties without the need for a TTP. The protocol combines oblivious transfer and visual cryptography to allow candidate and examiner to jointly generate a pseudonym that anonymises the candidates test without the need for the anonymiser. The pseudonym is revealed only to the candidate at testing. The formal analysis of the protocol in ProVerif proves that the protocol satisfies the same security requirements stated for WATA IV.

The specification of WATA without TTP sees four roles. These are obtained from WATA IV by partitioning the examiner role as administrator, examiner and invigilator so that both protocol design and analysis gain detail. As we consider a corrupted examiner who can deviate from any of its assigned tasks, it follows that any of its sub-roles can be corrupted as well.

Oblivious Transfer

Oblivious transfer schemes allow a chooser to pick some pieces of information from a set that a sender offers him, in such a way that (a) the sender does not learn which pieces of information the choosers picks, and (b) the chooser learns no more than the pieces of information he picks. Our enhanced protocol adopts Tzeng's oblivious transfer scheme [Tze04]. In Tzeng's scheme, the chooser commits to some elements from a set, and sends the commitments to the sender. This, in turn, obfuscates all the set's elements, and the chooser will be able to de-obfuscate only the elements he has committed to. Tzeng's scheme guarantees unconditional security for the receiver's choice, and it is efficient since it works with the sender and receiver's exchanging only two messages. This protocol uses oblivious transfer to avoid the participation of the honest-but-curious anonymiser seen in WATA IV.

Description

In this protocol, we mainly revise the preparation phase, while the design of the other phases are similar to the design of WATA IV. Candidate and examiner jointly generate the pseudonym *pid* as a pair of visual cryptography shares, by means of an oblivious transfer scheme rather than via the anonymiser. Notably, also the procedure for dispute resolution requires some modification since it cannot rely on the anonymiser's signatures.

The description of the protocol follows the four exam phases and implicitly assumes that all remote communications are via a secure channel. It also specifies the following public parameters:

n	length of the candidate's pseudonym
$\Sigma = \{s_1, \ldots, s_k\}$	alphabet of pseudonym's characters
$c_j \in \{0,1\}^{t \times u}$, $j = 1, \ldots, k$	$(t \times u)$-pixel representation of a character
idC	candidate ID
ex	exam code
SPK_A	signing key of the administrator
SPK_E	signing key of the examiner
M	set of possible marks
$g, h \in_{\mathcal{R}} \mathbb{G}_q$	generators for bit-commitments

1. C calculates $y_i = g^{x_i} h^{\gamma_i}$ where:

   - $x_i \in_\mathcal{R} \mathbb{Z}_q^*$.
   - $\gamma_i \in_\mathcal{R} [1, k]$.
   - $i = 1, 2, \ldots, l$ with $l > n$.

2. $C \rightarrow A$: $y_1, y_2, \ldots, y_l$.

3. A calculates $\beta_{ij} \leftarrow_{\pi_\mathcal{R}} (\alpha_i \oplus c_j)$, $\omega_{ij} = \langle a_{ij}, b_{ij} \rangle \leftarrow \langle g^{r_{ij}}, \beta_{ij} \left(\frac{y_i}{h^j} \right)^{r_{ij}} \rangle$,
   $com_A = h^s \prod\limits_{i=1}^{l} g_i{}^{\alpha_i}$, and $sign1 = Sign_{SSK_A}(idC, ex, com_A)$ where:

   - $\alpha_i \in_\mathcal{R} [0, 1]^{l \times u}$.
   - $s, r_{ij} \in_\mathcal{R} \mathbb{Z}_q^*$.
   - $g_i \in_\mathcal{R} \mathbb{G}_q$.
   - $i = 1, 2, \ldots, l$.
   - $j = 1, 2, \ldots, k$.

   or runs the challenge procedure against $y_1, y_2, \ldots, y_l$.

4. $A \rightarrow C$: $(\omega_{11}, \ldots, \omega_{1k}), \ldots (\omega_{l1}, \ldots, \omega_{lk})$ and $sign1$.

5. C calculates $\chi_i \in [1, l]$ and $\sigma_j \in [1, l]$ where:

   - $i = 1, 2, \ldots, m$.

6. $C \rightarrow A$: $\chi_1, \chi_2, \ldots, \chi_m$ and $\sigma_1, \sigma_2, \ldots, \sigma_n$.

7. A calculates $ev_{\chi_i} = \langle \alpha_{\chi_i}, (\beta_{\chi_i 1}, \beta_{\chi_i 2}, \ldots, \beta_{\chi_i k}), (r_{\chi_i 1}, r_{\chi_i 2}, \ldots, r_{\chi_i k}) \rangle$ and
   $sign2 = Sign_{SSK_A}(idC, ex, (y_{\sigma_1}, y_{\sigma_2}, \ldots, y_{\sigma_n}), (\alpha_{\chi_1}, \alpha_{\chi_2}, \ldots, \alpha_{\chi_m})$,
   $(\omega_{\sigma_1 1}, \ldots, \omega_{\sigma_1 k}), \ldots (\omega_{\sigma_n 1}, \ldots, \omega_{\sigma_n k})\}$ where

   - $i = 1, 2, \ldots, m$.
   - $j = 1, 2, \ldots, k$.

   and prints $\mathtt{transp} = \langle (\alpha_{\sigma_1}, \alpha_{\sigma_2}, \ldots, \alpha_{\sigma_n}), idC, ex, QR3 \rangle$ where

   - $QR3 = idC, ex, s$.

8. $A \rightarrow C$: $ev_{\chi_1}, ev_{\chi_2}, \ldots, ev_{\chi_m}$ and $sign2$.

9. C checks ev_{χ_i}, calculates $\beta_{\sigma_j} = \frac{b_{\sigma_j \gamma_j}}{(a_{\sigma_j \gamma_j})^{x_{\sigma_j}}}$ where

   - $i = 1, 2, \ldots, m$.
   - $j = 1, 2, \ldots, n$.

   and prints $\mathtt{paper} = \langle (\beta_{\sigma_1}, \beta_{\sigma_2}, \ldots, \beta_{\sigma_n}), idC, ex, QR1, QR2 \rangle$ where

   - $QR1 = idC, ex, sign1, com_A, (x_{\sigma_1}, x_{\sigma_2}, \ldots, x_{\sigma_n}), (\gamma_{\sigma_1}, \gamma_{\sigma_2}, \ldots, \gamma_{\sigma_n})$.
   - $QR2 = idC, ex, sign2, (y_{\sigma_1}, y_{\sigma_2}, \ldots, y_{\sigma_n}), (\alpha_{\chi_1}, \alpha_{\chi_2}, \ldots, \alpha_{\chi_m})$,
     $(\omega_{\sigma_1 1}, \ldots, \omega_{\sigma_1 k}), \ldots (\omega_{\sigma_n 1}, \ldots, \omega_{\sigma_n k})$.

10. $A \xrightarrow{hands} K$: $\mathtt{transp}, \mathtt{test}$

Figure 6.7: Preparation phase

11. $C \xrightarrow{hands} K$: id_doc

12. K checks id_doc

13. $K \xrightarrow{hands} C$: transp

14. C picks a random **test**, calculates $pid = (\alpha_1, \alpha_2, \ldots, \alpha_n) \oplus (\beta_1, \beta_2, \ldots, \beta_n)$ and
    if pid is unintelligible then C writes $\text{test}_{\texttt{filled}} = (questions, answers, pid)$ otherwise C runs the Dispute Resolution algorithm.

15. $C \xrightarrow{hands} K$: $\text{test}_{\texttt{filled}}$

Figure 6.8: Testing phase

16. $K \xrightarrow{hands} E$: $\text{test}_{\texttt{filled}}$

17. E calculates $sign_E = Sign_{SSK_E}(pid, answers, mark)$ where:

    - $mark \in M$.

18. $E \rightarrow A$: $pid, answers, mark, sign_E$

19. A calculates $c = g^v h^{mark}$ and $sign3 = Sign_{SSK_A}(pid, answers, c)$

    - $v \in_{\mathcal{R}} \mathbb{Z}_q^*$.

20. $A \rightarrow \mathcal{BB}$: $pid, answers, c, sign3$

Figure 6.9: Marking phase

21. $C \rightarrow A$: $(\beta_1, \beta_2, \ldots, \beta_n), pid, sign1, sign2, sign3$

22. A calculates $sign4 = Sign_{SSK_A}(idC, ex, pid, mark, v)$

23. $A \rightarrow C$: $idC, ex, pid, mark, v, sign4$

Figure 6.10: Notification phase

Preparation

The goal of preparation is to generate a candidate's pseudonym, which is a string of n characters taken from alphabet Σ, and to encode it into two visual cryptographic shares. No one can know the pseudonym until candidate and invigilator meet at testing, when the candidate learns her pseudonym by overlapping the administrator's share with hers. The underlying idea is that the candidate provides a commitment to an index into an array. The administrator fills the array with a secret permutation of the characters, and only when the two secrets are brought together is the selection of a character determined.

Part of this phase is inspired by one of the schemes used to print a secret, proposed by Essex *et al.* [ECHA09]. We tailor that scheme so that it can generate a pseudonym as detailed in Figure 6.7. This modification also supports the dispute resolution algorithm, as we shall see below. The main technical differences between our preparation phase and the original scheme to print a secret are: (a) a modified oblivious transfer protocol that copes with several secret messages in only one protocol run; (b) the generation of signatures that will be used for accountability in the resolution of disputes.

In the following, we refer to the steps described in Figure 6.7. The protocol begins with the candidate providing a sequence of l commitments y_i to an index into an array of length k (steps 1-2). More precisely, the parameter l is chosen so that the $l - n$ elements can be later used for a cut-and-choose audit. The administrator can challenge the candidate to check whether the committed choices are in fact in the interval $[1, k]$. Otherwise, the administrator generates a sequence of randomly chosen $t \times u$ images, indicated as $\alpha_1, \ldots, \alpha_l$ in Figure 6.7. A sequence of k images $\beta_{i1}, \ldots, \beta_{ik}$ are generated from α_i and each possible character c_j. The sequence is randomly permuted and repeated for all i, resulting in l sequences of images $(\beta_{11}, \ldots, \beta_{1k}), \ldots, (\beta_{l1}, \ldots, \beta_{lk})$. The secret permutation and the commitment allow the selection of a character to be determined only when the two secrets are brought together.

The administrator then generates the obfuscation ω_{ij} from each β_{ij} and a commitment on each α_i, indicated as *com* (step 3), which is signed and sent with the sequences of obfuscations $(\omega_{11}, \ldots, \omega_{1k}), \ldots, (\omega_{l1}, \ldots, \omega_{lk})$ to the candidate (step 4). The obfuscation allows the candidate to retrieve only the elements whose indexes correspond to the choices $y_1, \ldots, y_l$ she committed to in step 1.

The candidate performs a cut-and-choose audit, selecting a random set of $l - n$ sequences amongst the ω. By doing so, she can check whether the administrator generated the sequence of images correctly. The remaining substitutions $\sigma_1, \sigma_2, \ldots, \sigma_n$ select the indexes of the images that make the pseudonym. Thus, the visual share of the administrator consists of the concatenated images $\alpha_{\sigma_1}, \ldots, \alpha_{\sigma_n}$ (steps 5-6).

The administrator then generates the proofs for the cut-and-choose audit and prints the visual share and the candidate's details in the transparency printout **transp**. This also includes the secret value s used for the commitment of all the elements $\alpha_1, \ldots, \alpha_l$ (step 7). The secret value is represented in the form of a QR code. The administrator generates a signature that contains the candidate's commitments $y_1, \ldots, y_l$, the sequence of images used for the cut-and-choose audit $\alpha_1, \ldots, \alpha_m$, and the sequences of selected obfuscations $(\omega_{\sigma_1 1}, \ldots, \omega_{\sigma_1 k}), \ldots (\omega_{\sigma_n 1}, \ldots, \omega_{\sigma_n k})$. The administrator then sends the signature and the proofs to the candidate (step 8). In turn, the candidate checks the signature and the proofs, de-obfuscates the elements ω, and retrieves the visual share consisting of the concatenated image $\beta_{\sigma_1}, \beta_{\sigma_2}, \ldots, \beta_{\sigma_n}$. She finally prints the share, together with the two signatures, on a **paper** printout (step 9). At this point, both candidate and administrator have a visual share each; it is these two shares that, once overlapped, return an intelligible sequence of characters that serves as candidate's pseudonym.

The candidate's paper printout includes two QR codes (*QR1* and *QR2*) while the administrator's transparency only one (*QR3*). All these codes refer to the same candidate identity *idC* and exam identifier *ex*. The QR codes *QR1* and *QR2* notably encode the two signatures of the administrator respectively, while *QR3* encodes the secret value s. This phase concludes with the administrator handing the transparency to the invigilator (step 10).

Testing

The steps of this phase are described in Figure 6.8. The invigilator leaves a pile of tests on a desk at the exam venue. The candidate brings the paper printout at exam venue, while the invigilator brings the transparencies. The invigilator authenticates the candidate by checking her identity document (steps 11-12). He then gives the candidate her corresponding transparency and invites the candidate to pick a test randomly (steps 13-14). The candidate overlaps her paper printout with the transparency and learns her pseudonym, which she writes on the test. If no pseudonym appears, then this may happen only if the candidate or the administrator misprinted their printouts, and the Dispute Resolution algorithm outlined in Algorithm 1 reveals the principal that is accountable for the misbehaviour. At the end of the phase, the candidate returns the filled test by inserting it anywhere in the pile of tests (step 15), and takes both transparency and paper printouts home. The randomness exercised in dispatching the tests (to the candidates) and in returning the filled tests (to the invigilator) thwarts the risk that the invigilator builds visual associations between a test and a candidate.

Marking

At marking (see Figure 6.9), the invigilator hands the filled tests to an examiner (step 16). For each filled test, the latter evaluates the answers, assigns a mark, and generates a signature on the triplet formed by pseudonym, answers and mark (step 17). Then, the examiner sends the triplet and the signature to the administrator (step 18). The administrator generates a commitment on the assigned mark (step 19), signs pseudonym, answers, and the commitment, and finally publishes the signature on the bulletin board (step 20).

Notification

We refer to the steps described in Figure 6.10 for notification. This phase opens for a fixed time during which the candidate can remotely request to learn her mark and having it registered. She has to send the ordered sequences of $\beta_1, \ldots, \beta_n$, her pseudonym, and all the signatures she collected so far to the administrator (step 21). The administrator checks the signatures, overlaps the given sequence with the corresponding sequences of $\alpha_1, \ldots, \alpha_n$, and checks the pseudonym. Again, if no registered pseudonym appears, Dispute Resolution can reveal the principal who misbehaved. The administrator signs mark, pseudonym, and the secret parameter used to commit the mark (step 22), and sends the signature to the candidate (step 23). By doing so, the candidate can verify the correctness of the mark by looking at the bulletin board.

Data: Public parameters: $(C, n, g_i, h, idC, ex, SPK_A)$

- $paper = (\beta_{\sigma_1}, \beta_{\sigma_2}, \ldots, \beta_{\sigma_n}), idC, ex, sign1, sign2, (x_{\sigma_1}, x_{\sigma_2}, \ldots, x_{\sigma_n}),$
  $(\gamma_{\sigma_1}, \gamma_{\sigma_2}, \ldots, \gamma_{\sigma_n})$ where

  - $sign1 = Sign_{SSK_A}\{idC, ex, com_A\}.$
  - $sign2 = Sign_{SSK_A}\{idC, ex, (y_{\sigma_1}, y_{\sigma_2}, \ldots, y_{\sigma_n}), (\alpha_{\chi_1}, \alpha_{\chi_2}, \ldots, \alpha_{\chi_m}),$
    $(\omega_{\sigma_1 1}, \ldots, \omega_{\sigma_1 k}), \ldots (\omega_{\sigma_n 1}, \ldots, \omega_{\sigma_n k})\}.$

- $transp = (\alpha_{\sigma_1}, \alpha_{\sigma_2}, \ldots, \alpha_{\sigma_n}), idC, ex, s.$

Result: Corrupted participant(s)

if *sign1 is verifiable with SPK_A* **and** *sign2 is verifiable with SPK_A* **then**

    if $y_{\sigma_j} \neq g^{x_{\sigma_j}} h^{\gamma_{\sigma_j}}$ *or* $\beta_{\sigma_j} \neq \frac{b_{\sigma_j \gamma_j}}{(a_{\sigma_j \gamma_j})^{x_{\sigma_j}}}$ $[j = 1, 2, \ldots n]$ **then**

        if $com_A \neq h^s \prod_{i=1}^{l} g_i{}^{\alpha_i}$ **then**

        | **return** Administrator and Candidate

        else

        | **return** Candidate

    else

    | **return** Administrator

else

| **return** Candidate

Algorithm 1: Testing dispute resolution

6.5.1 Dispute Resolution

Algorithm 1 provides an efficient way to resolve a dispute if the candidate retrieves no intelligible pseudonyms when she overlaps the visual shares. We assume that an electronic device with a camera is available at the exam venue. It could be a smart phone or tablet, and it should store the public key of the administrator. The input of the algorithm are the two QR codes printed on the paper printout (QR1 and QR2) and the QR code printed on the transparency (QR3), all scanned with the camera of the electronic device. Note that the trustworthiness of dispute resolution comes from the correctness (soundness and completeness) of the algorithm, which is open to anyone for checking. Some trust is still required on the device used to resolve the dispute; however, it is always possible to run dispute resolution on any other device.

The goal of the algorithm is to reconstruct the correct visual shares, if possible. First, the algorithm checks the correctness of the signatures encoded in QR1 and QR2. If any of the checks fails, then the correct visual shares cannot be reconstructed. However, this reveals that the candidate misprinted her paper printout, thus she is the culprit. Otherwise, the algorithm reconstructs the correct visual share of the candidate by checking the candidate's commitments and the obfuscation — both signed by the administrator. If the check reveals that the reconstructed visual share matches the one printed by the candidate, then the culprit is the administrator. Otherwise, the algorithm reconstructs the administrator's visual share by checking the correctness of the administrator's commitment using the secret value encoded in QR3. If the check succeeds, then the candidate is the culprit, otherwise both candidate and examiner misprinted their visual shares.

6.5.2   Security of WATA Without TTP

We analyse the protocol in ProVerif. In the remainder, we first present the formal model, and then the results of the analysis of authentication, privacy, verifiability, and accountability requirements.

Model Choices

The model of TLS and face-to-face communications between the roles can be captured using the cryptographic primitive of probabilistic symmetric encryption rather than using ProVerif's private channels. The attacker cannot monitor communications via ProVerif's private channels and cannot even know if any communication takes place. This would be an overly strong assumption that could miss attacks. By renouncing to private channels, we achieve stronger security guarantees for the analysis of the protocol. Moreover, this choice has a triple advantage: i) it gives the attacker more discretional power because he can observe when a candidate registers for the exam, when she is given the test, when she submits the answers, and when she is notified with a mark; ii) it allows modelling either corrupted candidate or examiner by just sharing the private key with the attacker; iii) it increases the chances that verification attempts in ProVerif terminate.

The equational theory illustrated in Table 6.1 models the cryptographic primitives of the protocol. The theory for probabilistic symmetric key consists of two functions $senc$ and $sdec$. A message encrypted with a private key can only be decrypted using the same private key. Note that the randomness r on the encryption algorithm causes that the same message encrypted several times outputs different ciphertexts. The equational theory for the digital signature is rather standard in ProVerif.

Primitive	Equation
Prob. symmetric enc.	$sdec(senc(m, k, r), k) = m$
Digital signature	$getmess(sign(m, ssk)) = m$
	$checksign(sign(m, ssk), spk(ssk)) = m$
Oblivious transfer	$deobf(obf(r, m, \texttt{sel}, commit(r', \texttt{sel})), r') = m$
Visual cryptography	$overlap(share, gen\_share(m, share)) = m$
	$overlap(share, share) = share$

Table 6.1: Equational theory to model the enhanced protocol

We introduce a novel theory to model oblivious transfer and visual cryptography. The function *obf* allows the examiner to obfuscate the elements $\beta_1, \ldots, \beta_i$, while the function *deobf* returns the correct element β_{sel} to the candidate, depending on the choice she committed. We also provide the theory for the Pedersen commitment scheme with the function *commit*. Finally, we model the generation of a visual cryptography share with *gen_share*, and their overlapping with the function *overlap*.

In addition, we also model an unbounded number of corrupted candidates who can register for the exam. All the processes are augmented with the events that allow the verification of authentication requirements.

Anonymous Examiner is checked in presence of corrupted candidates and Anonymous Marking in presence of corrupted administrator, examiner and co-candidates, which means that the attacker can control an unbounded number of candidates while some are honest. To verify Question Indistinguishability, we consider corrupted candidates, while for both Mark Privacy and Mark Anonymity we consider corrupted eligible candidates who can register for the exam but cannot participate at testing.

To verify Mark Integrity Verifiability, we model the verifiability-test *testMI* as in Algorithm 2. It takes in, via a private channel, the pseudonym *pid*, the secret value *v*, and the mark notified to the candidate. It also takes as input the signed notification *sign3* containing the pseudonym, the answers, and the committed mark from the bulletin board. The verifiability-test checks if the administrator's signature is correct and the disclosure of the commitment contained in the signed notification reveals the mark provided by the candidate. We verify the soundness of the test in the presence of corrupted administrator, examiner, invigilator, and co-candidates. In the applied π-calculus, testMIV can be specified as a process that emits the event $OK(id\_c, pid, mark)$ when it is supposed to output *true* and KO otherwise. The event *published(pid)* is emitted by the bulletin board when a test identified with *pid* is available; the event *assigned(id_c, pid, mark)* is emitted by the candidate at the end of notification.

The verifiability-test *testTIV* depicted in Algorithm 3 takes in the pseudonym *pid* and the answer submitted by the candidate. It also takes as input the signed notification *sign3* containing the pseudonym, the answers and the committed mark from the bulletin board. The verifiability-test checks if the administrator's signature is correct and the signed answer matches the answer submitted by the candidate. We also verify the soundness of this test in the presence of corrupted administrator, examiner, invigilator, and co-candidates. In the applied π-calculus, testTIV can be specified as a process that emits the event $OK(id\_c, pid, answer)$ when it is supposed to output *true* and KO when it supposed to output *false*. The event *published(pid)* is emitted by the administrator when a test identified with *pid* is available; the event *accepted(id_c, pid, mark)* is emitted by the candidate at the end of marking.

Accountability

Below, we formally model Dispute Resolution in the applied π-calculus by appealing to a process **dispute** that performs dispute resolution. The definition relies on two caveats: first it resorts to unreachability of an event to prove soundness; second, as it may happen that *both* candidate and administrator are corrupted, it considers also this case towards soundness. The **dispute** process

Data: Public parameters: (g, h, SPK_A)

  - $sign3 = Sign_{SSK_A}(pid, answers, c)$

  - $idC, pid', mark, v$.

Result: Whether the candidate was notified with the mark assigned to
    her test.

if $pid = pid'$ **and** $c = g^v h^{mark}$ **then**

 | **return** *true*

else

 | **return** *false*

   Algorithm 2: The verifiability-test for Mark Integrity I.V.

Data: Public parameters: (g, h, SPK_A)

  - $sign3 = Sign_{SSK_A}(pid, answers, c)$

  - $idC, pid', answers', v$.

Result: Whether the candidate was notified with the mark assigned to
    her test.

if $pid = pid'$ **and** $answers = answers'$ **then**

 | **return** *true*

else

 | **return** *false*

  Algorithm 3: The verifiability-test for Test Integrity Verifiability

emits the event `Cguilty` when the candidate is the culprit, the event `Aguilty` if the administrator is the culprit, or the event `CAguilty` if both are culprits. If the protocol executes the process `dispute`, then at least either the administrator or the candidate is corrupted. Thus, assuming that `dispute` returns a principal, the idea is to check that `dispute` cannot return an honest principal, if any, instead of the corrupted one. For soundness, this is captured by the following definitions.

Definition 44 (Soundness of dispute resolution process) *The   dispute resolution process* `dispute` *is sound*

- *in case of corrupted administrator and honest candidate if it emits* `Cguilty` *and* `CAguilty` *in no execution trace of the exam protocol;*

- *in case of corrupted candidate and honest administrator if it emits* `Aguilty` *and* `CAguilty` *in no execution trace of the exam protocol;*

- *in case of corrupted administrator and candidate if it emits* `Cguilty` *and* `Aguilty` *in no execution trace of the exam protocol.*

To prove completeness, we check that the exam protocol never runs the process `dispute`, hence events `Cguilty`, `Aguilty`, and `CAguilty` are not emitted. This is captured by the following definition.

Definition 45 (Completeness of dispute resolution process) *The   dispute resolution process* `dispute` *is complete if it emits the events* `Aguilty`, `Cguilty`, *and* `CAguilty` *in no execution trace of the protocol with honest roles.*

Definition 46 (Testing Dispute Resolution) *An exam protocol ensures Dispute Resolution if the dispute resolution process* `dispute` *is sound and complete.*

Limitations

A limitation of the formal model is the specification of the cut-and-choose audit due to the powerful ProVerif's attacker model. In fact, if the attacker plays the cutter's role, he might cut the set of elements such that the subset audited by the chooser is correct, while the other subset is not. Although in reality the probability of success of this attack for a large set of elements is small, it is a valid attack in ProVerif irrespective of the number of elements. In our case, the chooser is the candidate, and the cutter is the examiner. ProVerif thus finds a false attack when the examiner is corrupted, namely controlled by the attacker. We resolve this false-positive by allowing the candidate to check all the elements of the set. This is sound because the candidate plays the role of the chooser, thus she is honest and follows the protocol although she knows the extra information.

Another limitation concerns the analysis of the soundness of dispute resolution with respect to corrupted administrator and candidate. The classic way to model the scenario of corrupted principals is to let the attacker control them. However, it can be observed that such a modelling does not work in this case because the conflicting goals of administrator and candidate are prerequisites for dispute resolution. Ideally, we would need administrator and candidate to be controlled by two different attackers that are only limited by the conflicting goals. A way to do so is to check the soundness of dispute resolution in the case of corrupted administrator and candidate by generating two correct printouts and by sharing both with the attacker. We then prove that if the attacker feeds dispute with any two printouts that are both different from the correct ones, the events Cguilty and Aguilty are emitted in no execution trace of the exam protocol.

Results

Table 6.2 outlines the results of our analysis and the execution times of ProVerif over an Intel Core i7 2.6 GHz machine with 8 GB RAM. ProVerif confirms that the protocol guarantees all the authentication requirements even under an unbounded number of corrupted, eligible co-candidates. Thus, the protocol ensures authentication although the attacker can register to the exam. Partitioning the examiner role as administrator, examiner and invigilator enables a finer analysis: we can prove in ProVerif that the protocol ensures most of the authentication requirements when considering both corrupted administrator and examiners. This would not be possible to prove in the setting of WATA IV. However, we cannot prove Candidate Authorisation and Mark Authentication because it is not possible to model in ProVerif the related correspondence assertions assuming corrupted administrators.

Regarding privacy, ProVerif proves that the protocol guarantees all the privacy requirements. In particular, the protocol meets Anonymous Marking considering corrupted administrator and examiner, and Anonymous Examiner considering corrupted candidates;

ProVerif confirms that the verifiability-tests $testMIV$ and $testTIV$ are sound and complete, thus it can be claimed that the exam protocol is Mark Integrity and Test Integrity verifiable.

Finally, the exam protocol ensures Dispute Resolution: ProVerif shows that the protocol does not blame honest principals when the dispute algorithm is executed or blames those who are corrupted (soundness). In particular, it blames both administrator and examiner when they are both corrupted. ProVerif also shows that the pseudonym is always revealed, namely the dispute algorithm is not run, when both examiner and candidate are honest (completeness).

6.6   Conclusion

This chapter draws its motivation by observing that exam security has a significant role in the widespread acceptance of computer-assisted exams. It focuses on a family of computer-assisted exams called WATA and shows how to gradually remove the need for trusted third party in their design, though ensuring more security requirements.

This chapter provides a new outlook of WATA II and WATA III, which originally were conceived as software running on the examiner's machine, by re-engineering them as exam protocols. It discusses their security properties, trust assumptions, and both security and functional limitations. Then, it discusses WATA IV, an exam protocol that allows both remote registration and remote notification. WATA IV reduces the participation of TTP respect to the previous versions significantly while guaranteeing more security requirements. Moreover, WATA IV supports both computer-based exam and traditional testing.

An enhancement of WATA IV results in a new protocol that meets the same security requirements for WATA IV but without the need for a TTP. The underlying idea is to combine oblivious transfer and visual cryptography to generate a pseudonym that anonymises the test for the marking. A formal analysis in ProVerif confirms that the enhanced protocol ensures all the stated requirements.

Finally, this chapter advances the accountability requirement of Dispute Resolution and its formal specification. The security analysis of the enhanced protocol in ProVerif confirms that it also meets this requirement without the need for a mediating TTP.

Requirement name	Result	Time
Candidate Authorisation	✓	6 s
Answer Authenticity	✓	5 s
Test Origin Authentication	✓	5 s
Test Authenticity	✓	6 s
Mark Authenticity	✓	6 s
Notification Request Auth.	✓	6 s
Mark Authentication	✓	6 s
Question Indistinguishability	✓	<1 s
Anonymous Marking	✓	1m 5s
Anonymous Examiner	✓	2 m 19 s
Mark Privacy	✓	32 m 23 s
Mark Anonymity	✓	9 m 12 s
Mark Integrity I.V.	✓	<1s
Test Integrity I.V.	✓	<1s
Dispute Resolution	✓	<1s

Table 6.2: Summary of the analysis of the enhanced protocol

Chapter 7

Conclusions

Running fair exams is the main way to achieve meritocracy in our society. This book argues that fair exams can be engineered by looking at how modern security cryptographic protocols are designed and analysed. Thus, a rigorous understanding of the security requirements of exams is fundamental to design protocols that withstand threats coming from malicious candidates and authorities. Moreover, it is necessary to develop formal approaches that permit us to prove that an exam protocol meets the stated security requirements. This book proposes formal methods for the security analysis of exams, and cryptographic techniques for the design.

It is found that two fundamental groups of requirements for exams are authentication and privacy. Authentication requirements aim to preserve the association between candidate identity, mark, and test throughout the entire examination. Privacy requirements aim to provide anonymity to both candidates and examiners. Exams should ensure verifiability as well, similarly to the end-to-end verifiability needed in voting systems. Exam protocols should provide enough information to allow candidates and auditors to verify the correctness of the exam using private and public available information.

The security of exams should be studied with adequate frameworks. Regarding the analysis of authentication and privacy, this book discusses a formal framework that enables the evaluation of exams specified in the applied π-calculus. The framework proves to be flexible as it supports various types of exams, namely traditional, computer-assisted, and Internet-based exams. Regarding the analysis of verifiability, the framework consists of an abstract model that supports a wide choice of verification methods based either on symbolic or on computational models. Both frameworks can be expanded with additional requirements. In Chapter 6, we extend both frameworks with the specification of Notification Request Authentication and Dispute Resolution.

This book details three protocols that demonstrate how the design of traditional, computer-assisted, and Internet-based exam can benefit from different cryptographic techniques such as exponentiation mixnet or visual cryptography. The protocols share the same design principle of minimising the reliance on the trusted third parties. The use of formal frameworks makes it possible to assess the security of the protocols.

Some interesting outcomes can be summarised. One is about the formal analysis of a secure exam protocol: it is observed that authentication can fail

© Springer International Publishing AG 2018

R. Giustolisi, *Modelling and Verification of Secure Exams*, Information Security and Cryptography, https://doi.org/10.1007/978-3-319-67107-9

because of the presence of logic flaws in the design of the protocol, while privacy can fail because the protocol relies upon inadequate cryptographic primitives. A second insight is about the relation between exams and similar domains, such as voting. The approaches for the analysis of those systems are similar; still, there are a few requirements that differ. Another interesting outcome concerns the possibility to design cryptographic exam protocols that meet contrasting requirements without the need for a TTP for both remote and face-to-face testing. Exams should not rely on TTP and should guarantee some forms of accountability.

The limit of this book is delineated by some choices related to security requirements and analysis approaches. The book treats the formalisation of authentication, privacy, and verifiability, but definitions of non-repudiation and accountability are also relevant for exams. The formalisation of Dispute Resolution goes in that direction. Another limiting choice is the list of considered requirements in each group. The elements of this list are highly desirable according to experience and discussions with colleagues. However, the list is not meant to be exhaustive: some exams may demand additional requirements, as is the case with WATA protocols.

The analysis inherits the limitations of ProVerif. Although the analysis is sound, ProVerif implements safe abstractions that might lead to non-termination or false attacks. The recourse to manual proofs may help to overcome some limitations, as in the case of the analysis of Remark! for universal verifiability.

In summary, this book has described the security requirements for exams, the frameworks for their analysis, and the design approach for exam protocols. The ideas discussed in this book may be useful for the modelling and verification of similar systems, such as for public tenders, project reviews, and conference management systems. By promoting a fairer assessment of knowledge and skills through the many application scenarios that award a qualification or a post to people, this line of research can significantly contribute to advancing modern meritocracy.

Future Work

Future work that continues the work presented in this book can be envisaged over different research directions.

Concerning the formal frameworks, it might be possible to extend them with the specification of new security requirements and to study the relation between the proposed requirements formally. Also, the analysis of more exam protocols would help to corroborate the flexibility of the proposed frameworks. In particular, it is interesting to analyse the verifiability of exams in the computational model, possibly with the assistance of automated tools like CryptoVerif [Bla08]. Another interesting research direction is to study whether the same approach described in this book to formalise verifiability for exams can be applied to check verifiability in voting systems.

Regarding Remark!, future work includes the extension of open-source platforms like Moodle with our protocol. Another interesting research direction is to expand Remark! with techniques to detect plagiarism and candidate cheating at testing. This research direction is significant because Remark! is designed to allow candidates to take the exam from home. We envisage that misbehaviour detection strategies such as data mining used to derive patterns described by

Pieczul and Foley [PF14] can be useful for this purpose. Another research direction includes the support for collaborative marking, in which the questions are categorised by subject, and examiners evaluate only the answers that pertain to the examiner subject area.

Future work can also be envisaged for computer-assisted exam protocols. One is to extend the proposed protocols to accommodate different exam scenarios. For instance, some scenarios may not require the participation of the candidate at notification. To achieve this, we envisage a temporal deanonymization solution similar to the one specified in Chapter 5 for Remark!. Dispute Resolution may conflict with the anonymity of the candidate's test. Thus it would be interesting to study how we can get the advantages of both of them in the design of exam protocols, and in general how to ensure both accountability and privacy requirements in the same system.

Another interesting line of research concerns the formal analysis. It might be possible to study compositional proofs that integrate computational proofs of the cryptographic primitives used in our protocol with the symbolic ones obtained in ProVerif. A practical research direction is the implementation of a prototype of the protocol and the verification of whether different visual cryptography schemes can be used to increase the perceptual security of an exam.

Bibliography

[ABB+05]   A. Armando, D. Basin, Y. Boichut, Y. Chevalier, L. Compagna, J. Cuellar, P. Hankes Drielsma, P. C. Heám, O. Kouchnarenko, J. Mantovani, S. Mödersheim, D. von Oheimb, M. Rusinowitch, J. Santiago, M. Turuani, L. Viganò, and L. Vigneron. The AVISPA Tool for the Automated Validation of Internet Security Protocols and Applications. In *Proceedings of the 17th International Conference on Computer Aided Verification*, CAV'05, pages 281–285, Berlin, Heidelberg, 2005. Springer-Verlag.

[ABR12]   Myrto Arapinis, Sergiu Bursuc, and Mark Ryan. Privacy Supporting Cloud Computing: ConfiChair, a Case Study. In *Proceedings of the First International Conference on Principles of Security and Trust*, POST'12, pages 89–108. Springer-Verlag, Berlin, Heidelberg, 2012.

[ABR13]   Myrto Arapinis, Sergiu Bursuc, and Mark Ryan. Privacy-supporting cloud computing by in-browser key translation. *J. Comput. Secur.*, 21(6):847–880, November 2013.

[ACC+08]   Alessandro Armando, Roberto Carbone, Luca Compagna, Jorge Cuellar, and Llanos Tobarra. Formal Analysis of SAML 2.0 Web Browser Single Sign-on: Breaking the SAML-based Single Sign-on for Google Apps. In *Proceedings of the 6th ACM Workshop on Formal Methods in Security Engineering*, FMSE '08, pages 1–10, New York, NY, USA, 2008. ACM.

[Adi08]   Ben Adida. Helios: Web-based open-audit voting. In *Proceedings of the 17th Conference on Security Symposium*, SS'08, pages 335–348, Berkeley, CA, USA, 2008. USENIX Association.

[AF01]   Martín Abadi and Cédric Fournet. Mobile values, new names, and secure communication. In *Proceedings of the 28th ACM SIGPLAN-SIGACT Symposium on Principles of Programming Languages*, POPL '01, pages 104–115, New York, NY, USA, 2001. ACM.

[AG97]   Martín Abadi and Andrew D. Gordon. A Calculus for Cryptographic Protocols: The Spi Calculus. *Proceedings of the 4th ACM Conference on Computer and Communications Security*, pages 36–47, 1997.

© Springer International Publishing AG 2018   129
R. Giustolisi, *Modelling and Verification of Secure Exams*, Information Security and Cryptography, https://doi.org/10.1007/978-3-319-67107-9

[AMRR14]   Myrto Arapinis, Loretta Ilaria Mancini, Eike Ritter, and Mark
            Ryan. Privacy through pseudonymity in mobile telephony sys-
            tems. In *21st Annual Network and Distributed System Security
            Symposium, NDSS 2014, San Diego, California, USA, February
            23-26, 2014*, 2014.

[BAN90]   Michael Burrows, Martin Abadi, and Roger Needham. A logic of
            authentication. *ACM Trans. Comput. Syst.*, 8(1):18–36, February
            1990.

[BCCKR11]   Giampaolo Bella, Gianpiero Costantino, Lizzie Coles-Kemp, and
            Salvatore Riccobene. Remote management of face-to-face written
            authenticated though anonymous exams. In *CSEDU*, pages 431–
            437. SciTePress, 2011.

[BCGL14]   Giampaolo Bella, Paul Curzon, Rosario Giustolisi, and Gabriele
            Lenzini. A socio-technical methodology for the security and pri-
            vacy analysis of services. In *2014 IEEE 38th International Com-
            puter Software and Applications Conference Workshops (COMP-
            SACW)*, pages 401–406, July 2014.

[BCR10]   Giampaolo Bella, Gianpiero Costantino, and Salvatore Riccobene.
            WATA - A System for Written Authenticated though Anonymous
            Exams. In *CSEDU (2)'10*, pages 132–137, 2010.

[Ben87]   Josh Benaloh. *Verifiable Secret-Ballot Elections*. PhD thesis, Yale
            University, September 1987.

[BGL13]   Giampaolo Bella, Rosario Giustolisi, and Gabriele Lenzini. What
            security for electronic exams? In *International Conference on
            Risks and Security of Internet and Systems (CRiSIS)*, October
            2013.

[BGW01]   Nikita Borisov, Ian Goldberg, and David Wagner. Intercepting
            mobile communications: The insecurity of 802.11. In *Proceedings
            of the 7th Annual International Conference on Mobile Computing
            and Networking*, MobiCom '01, pages 180–189, New York, NY,
            USA, 2001. ACM.

[BGZB09]   Gilles Barthe, Benjamin Grégoire, and Santiago Zanella Béguelin.
            Formal certification of code-based cryptographic proofs. In *Pro-
            ceedings of the 36th Annual ACM SIGPLAN-SIGACT Symposium
            on Principles of Programming Languages*, POPL '09, pages 90–
            101, New York, NY, USA, 2009. ACM.

[BHM08]   Michael Backes, Catalin Hritcu, and Matteo Maffei. Automated
            verification of remote electronic voting protocols in the applied pi-
            calculus. In *Proceedings of the 2008 21st IEEE Computer Security
            Foundations Symposium*, CSF '08, pages 195–209, Washington,
            DC, USA, 2008. IEEE Computer Society.

[Bla01]   Bruno Blanchet. An efficient cryptographic protocol verifier based
            on prolog rules. In *Proceedings of the 14th IEEE Workshop on*

Computer Security Foundations, CSFW '01, pages 82–, Washington, DC, USA, 2001. IEEE Computer Society.

[Bla08]   Bruno Blanchet. A computationally sound mechanized prover for security protocols. *IEEE Transactions on Dependable and Secure Computing*, 5(4):193–207, Oct 2008.

[BMU08]   Michael Backes, Matteo Maffei, and Domenique Unruh. Zero-knowledge in the applied pi-calculus and automated verification of the direct anonymous attestation protocol. In *IEEE Symposium on Security and Privacy, 2008. SP 2008.*, pages 202–215, May 2008.

[BRT13]   Josh Benaloh, Peter Y.A. Ryan, and Vanessa Teague. Verifiable postal voting. In *Security Protocols XXI*, volume 8263 of *Lecture Notes in Computer Science*, pages 54–65. Springer, Berlin, Heidelberg, 2013.

[BT94]   Josh Benaloh and Dwight Tuinstra. Receipt-free secret-ballot elections (extended abstract). In *Proceedings of the Twenty-sixth Annual ACM Symposium on Theory of Computing*, STOC '94, pages 544–553, New York, NY, USA, 1994. ACM.

[CF85]   Josh D. Cohen and Michael J. Fischer. A robust and verifiable cryptographically secure election scheme. In *Proceedings of the 26th Annual Symposium on Foundations of Computer Science*, SFCS '85, pages 372–382, Washington, DC, USA, 1985. IEEE Computer Society.

[Cha81]   David L. Chaum. Untraceable electronic mail, return addresses, and digital pseudonyms. *Communications of the ACM*, 24(2):84–90, February 1981.

[CJS+07]   Iliano Cervesato, Aaron D. Jaggard, Andre Scedrov, Joe-Kai Tsay, and Christopher Walstad. Breaking and fixing public-key kerberos. In *Advances in Computer Science - ASIAN 2006. Secure Software and Related Issues*, volume 4435 of *Lecture Notes in Computer Science*, pages 167–181. Springer, Berlin, Heidelberg, 2007.

[CLN09]   Cas J.F. Cremers, Pascal Lafourcade, and Philippe Nadeau. Comparing state spaces in automatic security protocol analysis. In *Formal to Practical Security*, volume 5458 of *Lecture Notes in Computer Science*, pages 70–94. Springer Berlin Heidelberg, 2009.

[Cop13]   Larry Copeland. School cheating scandal shakes up Atlanta. http://www.usatoday.com/story/news/nation/2013/04/13/atlanta-school-cheatring-race/2079327/, April 2013.

[Cou12]   Sean Coughlan. Harvard and MIT online courses get real world exams. http://www.bbc.com/news/education-19505776, September 2012.

[Cou15]   Coursera. Earn a Course Certificate. `https://www.coursera.org/signature/`, August 2015.

[CRHJDJ06] Jordi Castellà-Roca, Jordi Herrera-Joancomartí, and Aleix Dorca-Josa. A secure e-exam management system. In *ARES*, pages 864–871. IEEE Computer Society, 2006.

[DHL13]   J. Dreier, Jonker H., and P. Lafourcade. Defining verifiability in e-auction protocols. In *ASIACCS'13*, pages 547–552. ACM, 2013.

[DJL13]   Jannik Dreier, Hugo Jonker, and Pascal Lafourcade. Defining verifiability in e-auction protocols. In *ASIACCS*, pages 547–552. ACM, 2013.

[DJP10]   Naipeng Dong, Hugo L. Jonker, and Jun Pang. Analysis of a receipt-free auction protocol in the applied pi calculus. In *FAST'10*, volume 6561 of *LNCS*. Springer, 2010.

[DKR06]   Stephanie Delaune, Steve Kremer, and Mark Ryan. Coercion-resistance and receipt-freeness in electronic voting. In *Proceedings of the 19th IEEE Workshop on Computer Security Foundations*, CSFW '06, pages 28–42, Washington, DC, USA, 2006. IEEE Computer Society.

[DKR09]   Stephanie Delaune, Steve Kremer, and Mark D. Ryan. Verifying privacy-type properties of electronic voting protocols. *Journal of Computer Security*, 17(4):435–487, jul 2009.

[DLL12]   Jannik Dreier, Pascal Lafourcade, and Yassine Lakhnech. A formal taxonomy of privacy in voting protocols. In *Communications (ICC), 2012 IEEE International Conference on*, pages 6710–6715, June 2012.

[DLL13]   Jannik Dreier, Pascal Lafourcade, and Yassine Lakhnech. Formal verification of e-auction protocols. In David Basin and John C. Mitchell, editors, *Principles of Security and Trust*, volume 7796 of *Lecture Notes in Computer Science*, pages 247–266. Springer, Berlin, Heidelberg, 2013.

[DY83]   Danny Dolev and Andrew C. Yao. On the security of public key protocols. *IEEE Transactions on Information Theory*, 29(2):198–208, 1983.

[ECHA09]   Aleks Essex, Jeremy Clark, Urs Hengartner, and Carlisle Adams. How to print a secret. In *USENIX Conference on Hot Topics in Security*, HotSec. USENIX Association, 2009.

[EDTLR01]   Michael Elkins, David Del Torto, Raph Levien, and Thomas Roessler. MIME Security with OpenPGP. RFC 3156, 2001.

[EG85]   Tareq El Gamal. A public key cryptosystem and a signature scheme based on discrete logarithms. *IEEE Transactions on Information Theory*, 31(4):469–472, 1985.

[EKOT14]   Keita Emura, Akira Kanaoka, Satoshi Ohta, and Takeshi Taka-
           hashi. Building secure and anonymous communication channel:
           formal model and its prototype implementation. In *Symposium
           on Applied Computing, SAC 2014, Gyeongju, Republic of Korea -
           March 24 - 28, 2014*, pages 1641–1648. ACM, 2014.

[ETS15]   ETS. Tests and Products. https://www.ets.org/tests_
           products/alpha, July 2015.

[F99]   F. Javier Thayer Fábrega. Strand spaces: Proving security pro-
           tocols correct. *J. Comput. Secur.*, 7(2-3):191–230, March 1999.

[FGH+13]   Ana Ferreira, Rosario Giustolisi, Jean-Louis Huynen, Vincent
           Koenig, and Gabriele Lenzini. Studies in socio-technical security
           analysis: Authentication of identities with TLS certificates. In
           *Proceedings of the 2013 12th IEEE International Conference on
           Trust, Security and Privacy in Computing and Communications*,
           TRUSTCOM '13, pages 1553–1558, Washington, DC, USA, 2013.
           IEEE Computer Society.

[Fig14]   Le   Figaro.   Le   concours   de   médecine,   une
           sélection   impitoyable.   http://etudiant.
           lefigaro.fr/les-news/actu/detail/article/
           le-concours-de-medecine-une-selection-impitoyable-5428/,
           May 2014.

[FJ95]   Simon N. Foley and Jeremy L. Jacob. Specifying security for
           computer supported collaborative working. *Journal of Computer
           Security*, 3:233–253, 1995.

[FOK+98]   Steven Furnell, P. D. Onions, Martin Knahl, Peter W. Sanders,
           Udo Bleimann, U. Gojny, and H. F. Röder. A security frame-
           work for online distance learning and training. *Internet Research*,
           8(3):236–242, 1998.

[GFZN09]   Nataliya Guts, Cédric Fournet, and Francesco Zappa Nardelli.
           Reliable evidence: Auditability by typing. In Michael Backes
           and Peng Ning, editors, *Computer Security ESORICS 2009*, vol-
           ume 5789 of *Lecture Notes in Computer Science*, pages 168–183.
           Springer, Berlin, Heidelberg, 2009.

[GJ03]   Philippe Golle and Markus Jakobsson. Reusable anonymous re-
           turn channels. In *Proceedings of the 2003 ACM workshop on Pri-
           vacy in the electronic society*, WPES '03. ACM, 2003.

[GM82]   Joseph A. Goguen and José Meseguer. Security policies and secu-
           rity models. In *1982 IEEE Symposium on Security and Privacy,
           Oakland, CA, USA, April 26-28, 1982*, pages 11–20, 1982.

[GM84]   Shafi Goldwasser and Silvio Micali. Probabilistic encryption.
           Journal of Computer and System Sciences, 28(2):270 – 299, 1984.

[GMR85]   Shafi Goldwasser, Silvio Micali, and Charles Rackoff. The knowl-
           edge complexity of interactive proof-systems. In *Proceedings of the
           Seventeenth Annual ACM Symposium on Theory of Computing*,
           STOC '85, pages 291–304, New York, NY, USA, 1985. ACM.

[Gol96]   Dieter Gollmann. What do we mean by entity authentication?
           In *Proceedings of the 1996 IEEE Symposium on Security and Pri-
           vacy*, SP '96, pages 46–, Washington, DC, USA, 1996. IEEE Com-
           puter Society.

[Gop07]   Saravanan Gopinathan. Globalisation, the Singapore developmen-
           tal state and education policy: a thesis revisited. *Globalisation,
           Societies and Education*, 5(1):53–70, 2007.

[HCZ15]   Feng Hao, Dylan Clarke, and Avelino Francisco Zorzo. Delet-
           ing secret data with public verifiability. *Dependable and Secure
           Computing, IEEE Transactions on*, PP(99):1–1, 2015.

[HM05]   Changhua He and John C. Mitchell. Security analysis and im-
           provements for IEEE 802.11i. In *Proceedings of the Network and
           Distributed System Security Symposium, NDSS 2005, San Diego,
           California, USA*, 2005.

[HMPs14]   Susan Hohenberger, Steven Myers, Rafael Pass, and abhi shelat.
           Anonize: A large-scale anonymous survey system. In *Proceed-
           ings of the 2014 IEEE Symposium on Security and Privacy*, SP
           '14, pages 375–389, Washington, DC, USA, 2014. IEEE Computer
           Society.

[Hoa78]   Charles A. R. Hoare. Communicating Sequential Processes. *Com-
           mun. ACM*, 21(8):666–677, 1978.

[HP10]   Andrea Huszti and Attila Petho. A secure electronic exam system.
           Publicationes Mathematicae Debrecen, 77(3-4):299–312, 2010.

[HPC04]   Jordi Herrera-Joancomartí, Josep Prieto-Blázquez, and Jordi
           Castellà-Roca. A secure electronic examination protocol using
           wireless networks. In *International Conference on Information
           Technology: Coding and Computing (ITCC'04), Volume 2, April
           5-7, 2004, Las Vegas, Nevada, USA*, pages 263–268, 2004.

[HS00]   Martin Hirt and Kazue Sako. Efficient receipt-free voting based
           on homomorphic encryption. In *Proceedings of the 19th Inter-
           national Conference on Theory and Application of Cryptographic
           Techniques*, EUROCRYPT'00, pages 539–556, Berlin, Heidelberg,
           2000. Springer-Verlag.

[HS11]   Rolf Haenni and Olivier Spycher. Secure internet voting on lim-
           ited devices with anonymized DSA public keys. In *WOTE'11*.
           USENIX, 2011.

[Inc15]   ProctorU Inc. ProctorU - Online Proctoring. http://www.
           proctoru.com, August 2015.

[INF15]   INFOSAFE.   Anonymous   Marking.   http://www.
             anonymousmarking.com/, July 2015.

[KER09]   Michael Kazin, Rebecca Edwards, and Adam Rothman. *The
             Princeton Encyclopedia of American Political History. (Two vol-
             ume set)*. The Princeton Encyclopedia of American Political His-
             tory. Princeton University Press, 2009.

[KLP14]   Sudeep Kanav, Peter Lammich, and Andrei Popescu. A confer-
             ence management system with verified document confidentiality.
             In *Computer Aided Verification (CAV)*. 2014.

[KRS10]   Steve Kremer, Mark Ryan, and Ben Smyth. Election verifiability
             in electronic voting protocols. In *Proceedings of the 15th Euro-
             pean Conference on Research in Computer Security*, ESORICS'10,
             pages 389–404, Berlin, Heidelberg, 2010. Springer-Verlag.

[KTV10]   Ralf Küsters, Tomasz Truderung, and Andreas Vogt. Account-
             ability: Definition and relationship to verifiability. In *Proceedings
             of the 17th ACM Conference on Computer and Communications
             Security*, CCS '10, pages 526–535, New York, NY, USA, 2010.
             ACM.

[Lev04]   Adine Levine. Grading the Curve at HLS. http://hlrecord.
             org/?p=11168, November 2004.

[Lew13]   Tamar Lewin. Students Rush to Web Classes, but Profits May Be
             Much Later. https://nyti.ms/2jPTzy4, January 2013.

[Lip14]   Kevin   Liptak.   U.S.   Navy   discloses   nuclear   exam
             cheating.   http://edition.cnn.com/2014/02/04/us/
             navy-cheating-investigation/, February 2014.

[Low96]   Gavin Lowe. Breaking and Fixing the Needham-Schroeder Public-
             Key Protocol Using FDR. In *Proceedings of the Second Interna-
             tional Workshop on Tools and Algorithms for Construction and
             Analysis of Systems*, TACAS '96, pages 147–166, London, UK,
             1996. Springer-Verlag.

[Low97]   Gavin Lowe. A Hierarchy of Authentication Specifications. In
             *Proceedings of the 10th IEEE Workshop on Computer Security
             Foundations*, CSFW '97, pages 31–, Washington, DC, USA, 1997.
             IEEE Computer Society.

[Mea96]   Catherine Meadows. Language generation and verification in the
             NRL protocol analyzer. In *Computer Security Foundations Work-
             shop, 1996. Proceedings., 9th IEEE*, pages 48–61, Jun 1996.

[Mer83]   Michael John Merritt. *Cryptographic Protocols*. PhD thesis, At-
             lanta, GA, USA, 1983.

[Min14]   Ministère de l'éducation nationale de l'enseignement supérieur
             et de la recherche.   Statistiques du concours général
             des   lycées.   http://eduscol.education.fr/cid49775/

organisation-du-concours-general-des-lycees.html,
November 2014.

[Mou09]   Jean-Pierre Moussette. Method for anonymous computerized pro-
            cessing of documents or object. Patent, 08 2009. EP 1430439 B1.

[MPR13]   Matteo Maffei, Kim Pecina, and Manuel Reinert. Security and
            privacy by declarative design. In *Computer Security Foundations
            Symposium (CSF)*, pages 81–96. IEEE, 2013.

[MPW92]   Robin Milner, Joachim Parrow, and David Walker. A calculus
            of mobile processes. *Information and Computation*, 100(1):1–40,
            September 1992.

[Nee02]   Roger M. Needham. Back to the beginning. In *Security Protocols,
            10th International Workshop, Cambridge, UK, April 17-19, 2002,
            Revised Papers*, page 242, 2002.

[Neo15]   Neoptec. Nemo Scan: the reliable anonymity system. http://
            www2.neoptec.com/en/products/nemoscan/, July 2015.

[New15]   BBC News. Vyapam: India's deadly medical school exam scandal.
            http://www.bbc.com/news/world-asia-india-33421572, July
            2015.

[NS78]   Roger M. Needham and Michael D. Schroeder. Using encryption
            for authentication in large networks of computers. *Communica-
            tions of the ACM*, 21(12):993–999, December 1978.

[NS95]   Moni Naor and Adi Shamir. Visual cryptography. In *Advances
            in Cryptology EUROCRYPT'94*, volume 950 of *Lecture Notes in
            Computer Science*, pages 1–12. Springer Berlin Heidelberg, 1995.

[Off13]   European Personnel Selection Office. Careers with the Euro-
            pean Union. http:\europa.eu/epso/apply/how_apply/index_
            en.htm, November 2013.

[oS15]   The University of Sheffield. Marking policies and proce-
            dures. https://www.sheffield.ac.uk/scharr/current/pgt/
            marking, July 2015.

[Pau98]   Lawrence C. Paulson. The inductive approach to verifying crypto-
            graphic protocols. *Journal of Computer Security*, 6(1-2):85–128,
            January 1998.

[Pea15]   Pearson. Pearson VUE delivered exams. http://home.
            pearsonvue.com/test-taker/All-Tests.aspx, July 2015.

[Ped92]   Torben P. Pedersen. Non-interactive and information-theoretic
            secure verifiable secret sharing. In Joan Feigenbaum, editor,
            CRYPTO, LNCS, pages 129–140. Springer, 1992.

[PF14]   Olgierd Pieczul and Simon N. Foley. Collaborating as normal: de-
            tecting systemic anomalies in your partner. In *Proceedings of 22nd
            International Security Protocols Workshop, Cambridge*, 2014.

[Pre14]   Associated Press.   Navy kicks out 34 for nuke test
            cheating.   http://www.foxnews.com/us/2014/08/21/
            navy-kicks-out-34-for-nuke-cheating/, August 2014.

[Ros97]   Andrew W. Roscoe. *The Theory and Practice of Concurrency.*
            international series in computer science. Prentice-Hall, 1997.

[RS00]   Peter Y.A. Ryan and Steve Schneider. *The modelling and analysis*
            of security protocols: the CSP approach. Addison-Wesley Profes-
            sional, first edition, 2000.

[RS01]   Peter Y. A. Ryan and Steve A. Schneider. Process algebra and
            non-interference. *Journal of Computer Security*, 9(1-2):75–103,
            January 2001.

[RS06]   Peter Y. A. Ryan and Steve A. Schneider. Prêt à voter with re-
            encryption mixes. In *Proceedings of the 11th European conference*
            on Research in Computer Security, ESORICS'06, pages 313–326.
            Springer-Verlag, 2006.

[RS11]   Mark D. Ryan and Ben Smyth. Applied pi calculus. In *Formal*
            Models and Techniques for Analyzing Security Protocols, chap-
            ter 6. IOS Press, 2011.

[RT10]   Blake Ramsdell and Sean Turner. Secure/Multipurpose Inter-
            net Mail Extensions (S/MIME) Version 3.2 Message Specification.
            RFC 5751, 2010.

[Sch98]   Steve Schneider. Verifying authentication protocols in CSP. *IEEE*
            Transactions on Software Engineering, 24(9):741–758, Sep 1998.

[Sch15]   Stanford Law School.   Exams and Papers.   http:
            //www.law.stanford.edu/organizations/offices/
            office-of-the-registrar/exam-information, July 2015.

[Sha79]   Adi Shamir. How to share a secret. *Communications of the ACM*,
            22(11):612–613, 1979.

[SRKM10]   Ben Smyth, Mark Ryan, Steve Kremer, and K. Mounira. Towards
            automatic analysis of election verifiability properties. In *ARSPA-*
            WITS'10, volume 6186 of *LNCS*, pages 146–163. Springer, 2010.

[SS96]   Steve Schneider and Abraham Sidiropoulos. CSP and anonymity.
            In *Computer Security · ESORICS 96*, volume 1146 of *Lecture Notes*
            in Computer Science, pages 198–218. Springer, Berlin, Heidelberg,
            1996.

[TOE]   Test of English as a Foreign Language. http://www.ets.org/
            toefl.

[Tze04]   Wen-Guey Tzeng. Efficient 1-out-of-n oblivious transfer schemes
            with universally usable parameters. *IEEE Transactions on Com-*
            puters, 53(2):232–240, 2004.

[Uni15]   Dublin City University. Anonymous Marking. `http://www4.dcu.ie/iss/am/index.shtml`, July 2015.

[vDMR08]   Tony van Deursen, Sjouke Mauw, and Sasa Radomirović. Untraceability of RFID protocols. In *Information Security Theory and Practices. Smart Devices, Convergence and Next Generation Networks (WISTP'08)*, volume 5019 of *Lecture Notes in Computer Science*, pages 1–15. Springer, 2008.

[Wat14]   Robert Watson. Student visa system fraud exposed in BBC investigation. `http://www.bbc.com/news/uk-26024375`, February 2014.

[Wei05]   Edgar Weippl. *Security in E-learning*, volume 6 of *Advances in Information Security*. Springer, 2005.

[WL93]   Thomas Y.C. Woo and Simon S. Lam. A semantic model for authentication protocols. In *Research in Security and Privacy, 1993. Proceedings., 1993 IEEE Computer Society Symposium on*, pages 178–194, May 1993.

[YP13]   Li Yuan and Steven Powell. MOOCs and Open Education: Implications for Higher Education: A White Paper. Technical report, JICS - Centre for Educational Technology & Interoperable Standards (CETIS), 2013.

Printed in the United States
By Bookmasters